PARLIAMENTARY HISTORY: TEXTS & STUDIES

1

Peerage Creations

Chronological Lists of Creations in the
Peerages of England and Great Britain
1649–1800 and of Ireland 1603–1898

Parliamentary History: Texts & Studies

Peerage Creations

Chronological Lists of Creations in the
Peerages of England and Great Britain
1649–1800 and of Ireland 1603–1898

compiled by

J. C. Sainty

Wiley-Blackwell

For

The Parliamentary History Yearbook Trust

This edition first published 2008

© 2008 The Parliamentary History Yearbook Trust

Blackwell Publishing was acquired by John Wiley & Sons in February 2007. Blackwell's publishing programme has been merged with Wiley's global Scientific, Technical, and Medical business to form Wiley-Blackwell.

Registered Office

John Wiley & Sons Ltd, The Atrium, Southern Gate, Chichester, West Sussex, PO19 8SQ, United Kingdom

Editorial Offices

350 Main Street, Malden, MA 02148-5020, USA

9600 Garsington Road, Oxford, OX4 2DQ, UK

The Atrium, Southern Gate, Chichester, West Sussex, PO19 8SQ, UK

For details of our global editorial offices, for customer services, and for information about how to apply for permission to reuse the copyright material in this book please see our website at www.wiley.com/wiley-blackwell.

The right of J.C. Sainty to be identified as the compiler of the editorial material in this work has been asserted in accordance with the Copyright, Designs and Patents Act 1988.

Wiley also publishes its books in a variety of electronic formats. Some content that appears in print may not be available in electronic books.

Library of Congress Cataloging-in-Publication Data

Sainty, John Christopher.

Peerage creations : chronological lists of creations in the peerages of England and Great Britain, 1649–1800, and of Ireland, 1603–1898 / compiled by J.C. Sainty.

p. cm. – (Parliamentary history : texts & studies)

Includes bibliographical references and index.

ISBN 978-1-4051-8043-6 (pbk. : alk. paper)   1. Titles of honor and nobility–Great Britain.   2. Titles of honor and nobility–Ireland.   I. Parliamentary History Yearbook Trust.   II. Title.

CR3895.S25 2008

929.7094–dc22

2008015532

ISBN 987-1-4051-8043-6

A catalogue record for this title is available from the British Library

Set in 10/12pt Bembo

by SNP Best-set Typesetter Ltd., Hong Kong

Printed and bound in Singapore

by Hó Printing Pte Ltd

CONTENTS

Contents

EDITORIAL

It is ten years since the Parliamentary History Yearbook Trust first published J. C. Sainty's highly useful, *Peerage Creations, 1649–1800: A Chronological List of Creations in the Peerages of England and Great Britain*. This year, to mark the launch of the Trust's new series, *Parliamentary History: Texts & Studies*, we have returned to Sainty. This comprehensive volume bundles a revised and updated edition of Sainty's 1998 publication with his new research on Irish peerage creations. By extending our knowledge of peerage creations between 1649 and 1800, we believe that this volume will become the essential reference text for anyone working on the peerage.

The *Parliamentary History: Texts & Studies* series draws upon the interests and research of recent and established scholars to explore the parliamentary histories of England, Scotland and Ireland, broadly defined, and the changing nature of British political culture. The Parliamentary History Record Series will be replaced by the new series, which will publish significant monographs on political/parliamentary subjects, as well as carefully edited and fully noted volumes of primary-source documents.

The new series seeks to make parliamentary history more accessible to a wider, international audience. We are pleased to announce that, as part of our agreement with Wiley-Blackwell, subscribers to *Parliamentary History* will receive a volume of *Parliamentary History: Texts and Studies* each year as part of their subscription. The volumes will also be available to subscribers electronically through Blackwell Synergy. This year, to celebrate the move to Wiley-Blackwell, subscribers will receive two volumes of *Parliamentary History: Texts & Studies*: Sainty (volume 1) is being distributed free, to thank subscribers for their continued support of the journal, whereas Hannes Kleineke's *Parliamentarians at Law: Select Legal Proceedings of the Long Fifteenth Century Relating to Parliament* (volume 2) will be circulated to subscribers in 2008 as part of their subscription.

Enquiries about the series, and about the opportunities it provides for electronic publication, are welcome. Please contact the Series Editor at the School of Historical & Cultural Studies, Bath Spa University, Newton Park, Bath BA2 9BN.

Elaine Chalus

ABBREVIATIONS

B.	Barony
Bart.	Baronet
Chas.	Charles
D.	Dukedom
E.	Earldom
(E)	Peerage of England
(GB)	Peerage of Great Britain
Geo.	George
(I)	Peerage of Ireland
Jas.	James
Kt.	Knight
LP	Letters patent
M.	Marquessate
Mar.	Mary
P.	Prince
(S)	Peerage of Scotland
V.	Viscountcy
Will.	William

REFERENCES

Manuscript

Bodleian Library, Oxford
   Ashmole MS 838   Third volume of Peers' Patents 1658–74 collected by
                                        Elias Ashmole

The National Archives, London
   C 66   Chancery: Patent Rolls
   C 82   Chancery: Warrants for the Great Seal, series II
   C 231   Chancery: Crown Office Docket Books
   E 403/2462–2467   Exchequer: Auditor's Patent Books 1660–83
   E 403/2527   Exchequer: Pells Patent Book 1669–72

Printed works

Baronage   W. Dugdale, *The Baronage of England* (2 vols, 1675–6)

CP   *Complete Peerage*, ed. G.E.C. (2nd edn, 14 vols, 1910–98)

Introduction

The following list has two principal purposes: to provide a chronological account of creations in the peerages of England and Great Britain from the accession of Charles II in 1649 to the union with Ireland on 1 January 1801 and at the same time to correct errors which have found their way into standard reference works, notably the *Complete Peerage*.

Some explanation is required for adding to the already large literature on the peerage.[1] Culminating in the *Complete Peerage* (1910–98) most accounts have been constructed on the alphabetical principle which undoubtedly makes for ease of reference. However, these works suffer from the drawback that they do not enable the enquirer readily to discern changes in the frequency and character of peerage creations over time. This object can only be satisfactorily achieved by adopting the chronological method. Furthermore, it does not appear that the compilers of these works, at least for the period in question, undertook a systematic survey of the the documents of creation with the result that they have incorporated or perpetuated numerous errors, mainly in the dating of those documents.

As early as 1786 Robert Beatson provided in his *Political Index* a list of 'NOBILITY created from the Year 1067 to the Year 1786'.[2] This made no attempt at precise dating but is a tolerably accurate account of creations made in the later 17th and 18th centuries. In 1819 the house of lords published the texts of charters and letters patent of creation from the reign of Stephen to the death of Edward IV in 1483 in chronological sequence.[3] This undertaking was continued in 1886 in the *Report of the Deputy Keeper of Public Records* which listed creations from Richard III to Charles I (1483–1646).[4] This was based on original sources but is in concise form and does not include texts of the documents of creation. Lists covering the periods 1702–83 and 1784–1837, compiled by Professor Turberville, were published in 1927 and 1958 respectively.[5] Turberville does not appear to have used original sources for his lists which contain a number of errors and omissions.

Since Turberville's lists, which in any event do not cover the years 1649–1702, cannot be regarded as reliable it has been considered desirable to continue, in modified form, the deputy keeper's list of 1886 from the point where it left off until the union with Ireland when the peerage of Great Britain was replaced by that of the United Kingdom,

---

[1] For an account of earlier compilations, see F.-J. French, 'Debrett: Book and Man; A History of the Peerage', *Debrett's Peerage and Baronetage* (1990), pp. 14–20. I am indebted to Mr David L. Jones for this reference.

[2] R. Beatson, *A Political Index to the Histories of Great Britain and Ireland* (Edinburgh, 1786), pt. I, pp. 10–91.

[3] *Reports from the Lords Committees appointed to search the Journals of the House, Rolls of Parliament, and other Records and Documents for all matters touching the Dignity of a Peer of the Realm, &c, presented to the House 12 July 1819*, Appendix 2.

[4] *47th Report of the Deputy Keeper of Public Records* (1886), Appendix 6.

[5] A. S. Turberville, *The House of Lords in the XVIIIth Century* (1927), Appendix A; *The House of Lords in the Age of Reform* (1958), Appendix 3.

including for the sake of completeness the two creations made by Protector Oliver. It may be helpful to indicate the respects in which this list differs from its predecessor. The deputy keeper's list included creations in the peerage of Ireland insofar as the relevant letters patent were passed under the great seal of England. Irish peerages have been omitted from the present list although some continued to be created in this fashion until the reign of Anne.[6] Unlike that of 1886 this list does not include 'creations' by writ whether in acceleration or otherwise or instances where abeyances were terminated by letters patent. Nor does it record restorations of forfeited titles or the appointment of earls marshal. Finally it omits titles conferred in a less formal manner than by letters patent. Thus the creations of two of the sons of James II as dukes of Cambridge (1664, 1667) are included but the informal 'designations' of three other sons as dukes are omitted. Similarly omitted is the son of Queen Anne who, although designated duke of Gloucester, was never so created by letters patent.[7]

The principal sources on which the list is based are twofold: the crown office docket books and the patent rolls preserved in the National Archives. The docket books[8] were kept by the clerk of the crown in chancery and record in chronological sequence the issue of certain documents passed under the great seal including grants of peerages of England and after 1707 of Great Britain. The docket books minute the date and contents of each patent in summary form. As a general rule the full texts of the patents themselves were enrolled on the patent rolls.[9]

For the period of Charles II's exile (1649–60) no docket books or patent rolls exist although in two cases the texts of peerage patents issued during this period were enrolled after the Restoration.[10] For the rest information has to be sought from Dugdale's *Baronage*[11] and from the manuscript list of creations 1658–74 compiled by Elias Ashmole.[12] The issue of the two Cromwellian peerage patents are recorded in the docket book for the interregnum[13] but the patents themselves are not enrolled.

From the Restoration in May 1660 a complete sequence of docket books survives.[14] Generally speaking they have been taken as authoritative for the dating of creations. In only three cases does there appear to be a case for departing from the information which they provide.[15] From the same date the practice of enrolment was resumed but operated

---

[6] The last peerage of Ireland so created was the viscountcy of Castlecomer (1707) (C 231/9, p. 154). However, in eight later cases during the period peerages of Ireland were granted as subsidiary honours in the same patents that created higher titles in the peerage of Great Britain: the earldom of Ulster in association with the dukedom of York and Albany (1716, 1760, 1764); the earldom of Connaught in association with that of Gloucester and Edinburgh (1764); the earldom of Dublin with those of Cumberland and Strathearn (1766) and Kent and Stratheran (1799); the earldom of Munster with that of Clarence and St Andrews (1789); and the earldom of Armagh with that of Cumberland and Teviotdale (1799).

[7] For these designations, see *CP*, ii, 496–7; *ibid.*, v, 743; *ibid.*, vii, 111.

[8] C 231/6–13.

[9] C 66.

[10] Langdale (1658) and St. Albans (1660).

[11] This appears to be the only source for the creations of Wotton (1650) and Rochester (1652).

[12] Bodleian Library, Ashmole MS 838. This is the source for the creations of Crofts and Berkeley (1658), Gloucester and Mordaunt (1659).

[13] C 231/6.

[14] The first in this sequence (C 231/7) begins only on 29 May.

[15] See the cases of Griffin (1688), Tankerville and Howland (1695).

erratically at first. Between the Restoration and the death of Charles II in February 1685, 95 peerage patents were issued. In respect of these 21 enrolments have not been traced. However, from the accession of James II in 1685 and the Union in 1801 all of the 421 peerage patents issued are enrolled with the single exception of that creating the earldom of Jersey (1697).

To some extent the deficiencies of the patent rolls can be made good from other sources. Some patents were entered in the exchequer books because until the death of William III all peers above the rank of baron were granted annuities on their creation.[16] This source yields the texts of four patents not enrolled.[17] The texts of nine others can be recovered from Ashmole's list whether in the form of letters patent, usually abbreviated, or privy seal warrants.[18] The substance of four more exist in the second series of warrants for the great seal.[19] In the case of the earldom of Berkeley (1679) the original letters patent are preserved in the Parliamentary Archives. Apparently in only three cases is the text not available in some form.[20]

It is important to stress that the date of the enrolled patent cannot always be relied upon as evidence for the true date of creation, mainly for two reasons. In the first place, patents were on occasion entered on a roll for the wrong regnal year. This occurred in 18 cases during the period.[21] Secondly, the date to which the patent is attributed is sometimes at odds with that recorded in the docket book. Insofar as this was not a simple mistake the reason appears to be that those responsible for the enrolment selected the date by reference to the authorizing document rather than the issue of the patent. This conjecture derives some support from the fact that in some instances the text entered on the roll was that of the warrant and not the patent.[22]

In addition to details of creation the list provides information about the destination of each peerage and specifies those cases in which the limitation in remainder was other than to heirs male of the body. Where the patent in addition extends the remainder to a title previously granted this fact is noted.[23] Also included in the list is the only case of a patent issued solely for the purpose of such an extension.[24]

In summary the list is designed to provide the following information:

1. The date of creation. In principle the list contains all new creations in the peerages of England and Great Britain 1649–1800. However, it includes two exceptional cases. The patent of 11 December 1665 did not create a new peerage but, as mentioned in note 24, simply extended the remainder of an existing barony. Because the creation

---

[16] E 403/2462–2467, 2527. The last peerage patent to include provision for an annuity appears to be that creating the earldom of Grantham (1698).

[17] Brecknock (1660), Craven and Burlington (Mar. 1665), Cambridge (1667).

[18] Chesterfield (1660), St Liz, Arlington, Newcastle, Frescheville, Falmouth, Arundell (1665), Cleveland (1670), Duras (1673).

[19] C 82; Howard (1669), Southampton and Grafton (1675), Corbet (1679).

[20] Feversham (1676), Conway (1679), Jersey (1697).

[21] C 66/3081, no. 7 (1665); C 66/3607, no. 6 (1742); C 66/3782, nos. 12–18 (1780); C 66/3863, no. 13 (1790); C 66/3943, nos. 10–17 (1797).

[22] C 66/3825, no. 13 (1786); C 66/3830, nos. 10–19 (1786).

[23] Craven (Mar. 1665), Cowper and Cobham (1718).

[24] Craven (Dec. 1665).

of the barony of Morden (1770) is entered in the docket book it is included although the letters patent were not sealed due to the death of the grantee. The year is taken to have begun on 1 January throughout the period.

2. The principal title conferred (capitalized), followed by any other titles granted in descending order of rank. As mentioned in note 6 certain subsidiary titles in the peerage of Ireland are also included. For the spelling of titles the usage of the *Complete Peerage* has been adopted.

3. The name of the grantee. Where the grantee was a peer of Scotland or Ireland and possessed a peerage of England or Great Britain this fact is stated.

4. In cases where the remainder was other than to heirs male of the body of the grantee, details of the remainder. Where the patent extended the remainder to a dignity conferred earlier this fact is noted. In the list the term 'heirs male' should be construed as 'heirs male of the body'.

5. The sources from which the information is derived. Listed first is the reference to the docket book, where this is available, followed by the reference to the enrolment on the patent roll, noting any instance in which the date differs from that in the docket book; failing the patent roll to any source where the text or substance of the patent may be found.

6. An indication of instances in which the information given in the list differs from that provided by the *Complete Peerage*.

Creations 1649–1800

Charles II

1650 31 Aug.
    WOTTON, B.
    Charles Henry Kirkhoven.
    No enrolment traced; for creation, see *Baronage*, ii, 475.

1652 13 Dec.
    ROCHESTER, E.; Wilmot, V.
    Henry Lord Wilmot.
    No enrolment traced; for creation, see *Baronage*, ii, 469.

1658 4 Feb.
    LANGDALE, B.
    Sir Marmaduke Langdale, Kt.
    For LP 10 Chas. II, see Ashmole MS 838, pp. 3–4;
    enrolled 13 Chas. II, pt. 46 (C 66/3001) no. 14.

1658 18 May
    CROFTS, B.
    William Crofts.
    No enrolment traced; for LP 10 Chas. II, see Ashmole MS 838, pp. 1–2.

1658 19 May
    BERKELEY, B.
    Sir John Berkeley, Kt.
    No enrolment traced; for LP 10 Chas. II, see Ashmole MS 838, pp. 12–13.

1659 13 May
    GLOUCESTER, D.; Cambridge, E.
    Prince Henry.
    No enrolment traced; for LP 11 Chas. II, see Ashmole MS 838, pp. 9–11.

1659 10 July
    MORDAUNT, V.; Mordaunt, B.
    Hon. John Mordaunt.
    No enrolment traced; for LP 11 Chas. II, see Ashmole MS 838, pp. 7–8.

1660 27 Apr.
    ST. ALBANS, E.
    Henry Lord Jermyn.
    LP enrolled 12 Chas. II, pt. 40 (C 66/2955) no. 7.

1660 29 May   **CHESTERFIELD, E.**
                            Catherine Lady Stanhope.
                            For life.
                            No enrolment traced; for LP 12 Chas. II, see Ashmole
                            MS 838, pp. 14–15.

1660 7 July   **ALBEMARLE, D.**; Torrington, E.; Monck, B.
                            George Monck.
                            C 231/7, p. 13; 12 Chas. II, pt. 6 (C 66/2921) no. 13.

1660 12 July   **SANDWICH, E.**; Hinchingbrooke, V.;
                            Montagu, B.
                            Edward Montagu.
                            C 231/7, p. 18; 12 Chas. II, pt. 8 (C 66/2923) no. 9.

1660 14 July   **GUILDFORD, E.**
                            Elizabeth Viscountess Kinalmeaky.
                            For life.
                            C 231/7, p. 19; 12 Chas. II, pt. 17 (C 66/2932) no. 12.

1660 20 July   **BRECKNOCK, E.**; Butler, B.
                            James Marquess of Ormond (I).
                            C 231/7, p. 18; no enrolment traced; for LP, see
                            E 403/2462, ff. 51–52v.

1660 26 July   **FITZHERBERT, B.**
                            Heneage Earl of Winchilsea.
                            C 231/7, p. 20; 12 Chas. II, pt. 9 (C 66/2924) no. 12;
                            dated 26 June (*sic*) in *CP*, ii, 777.

1660 3 Nov.   **HYDE, B.**
                            Sir Edward Hyde, Kt.
                            C 231/7, p. 49; 12 Chas. II, pt. 11 (C 66/2926) no. 6.

1661 20 Apr.   **CLARENDON, E.**; Cornbury, V.
                            Edward Lord Hyde.
                            C 231/7, p. 98; 13 Chas. II, pt. 45 (C 66/3000) no. 21.

1661 20 Apr.   **ESSEX, E.**; Malden, V.
                            Arthur Lord Capell.
                            Remainder, failing heirs male, to brothers Hon. Henry
                            Capell and Hon. Edward Capell and heirs male
                            respectively.
                            C 231/7, p. 98; 13 Chas. II, pt. 45 (C 66/3000) no. 20.

1661 20 Apr.   **CARDIGAN, E.**
                       Thomas Lord Brudenell.
                       C 231/7, p. 98; 13 Chas. II, pt. 45 (C 66/3000) no. 15.

1661 20 Apr.   **ANGLESEY, E.**; Annesley, B.
                       Arthur Viscount Valentia (I).
                       C 231/7, p. 98; 13 Chas. II, pt. 45 (C 66/3000) no. 19.

1661 20 Apr.   **BATH, E.**; Lansdowne, V.; Granville, B.
                       Sir John Granville, Kt.
                       C 231/7, p. 98; 13 Chas. II, pt. 45 (C 66/3000) no. 16.

1661 20 Apr.   **CARLISLE, E.**; Morpeth, V.; Dacre, B.
                       Charles Howard.
                       C 231/7, p. 98; 13 Chas. II, pt. 45 (C 66/3000) no. 11;
                       dated 30 Apr. (*sic*) in *CP*, iii, 34.

1661 20 Apr.   **HOLLES, B.**
                       Hon. Denzil Holles.
                       C 231/7, p. 99; 13 Chas. II, pt. 45 (C 66/3000) no. 14.

1661 20 Apr.   **CORNWALLIS, B.**
                       Sir Frederick Cornwallis, Bart.
                       C 231/7, p. 99; 13 Chas. II, pt. 45 (C 66/3000) no. 18.

1661 20 Apr.   **DELAMER, B.**
                       Sir George Booth, Bart.
                       C 231/7, p. 99; 13 Chas. II, pt. 45 (C 66/3000) no. 17.

1661 20 Apr.   **TOWNSHEND, B.**
                       Sir Horatio Townshend, Bart.
                       C 231/7, p. 99; 13 Chas. II, pt. 45 (C 66/3000) no. 13.

1661 20 Apr.   **ASHLEY, B.**
                       Sir Anthony Ashley Cooper, Bart.
                       C 231/7, p. 99; 13 Chas. II, pt. 45 (C 66/3000) no. 12.

1661 20 Apr.   **CREW, B.**
                       John Crew.
                       C 231/7, p. 99; 13 Chas. II, pt. 45 (C 66/3000) no. 10.

1663 14 Feb.   **MONMOUTH, D.**; Doncaster, E.; Scott, B.
                       Sir James Scott, Kt.
                       C 231/7, p. 194 *bis*; 15 Chas. II, pt. 1 (C 66/3032)
                       no. 6.

1663 7 May

LUCAS, B.
Mary Countess of Kent.
Remainder to heirs male by husband Anthony Earl of Kent, whom failing, to heirs of body by same, with provision barring abeyance.
    C 231/7, p. 203; 15 Chas. II, pt. 1 (C 66/3032) no. 2.

1664 23 Aug.

CAMBRIDGE, D.; Cambridge, E.; Dauntsey, B.
James Stuart son of James Duke of York.
    C 231/7, p. 240; 16 Chas. II, pt. 7 (C 66/3057) no. 3.

1665 2 Feb.

ST. LIZ, B.
Basil Earl of Denbigh.
Remainder, failing heirs male, to heirs male of William late Earl of Denbigh.
    C 231/7, p. 251; no enrolment traced; for abbreviated LP, see Ashmole MS 838, p. 100.

1665 14 Mar.

ARLINGTON, B.
Sir Henry Bennet, Kt.
    C 231/7, p. 256; no enrolment traced; for abbreviated LP, see Ashmole MS 838, pp. 101–2. *CP*, i, 217 states in error that remainder extended to heirs of body, failing heirs male.

1665 16 Mar.

NEWCASTLE UPON TYNE, D.; Ogle, E.
William Marquess of Newcastle.
    C 231/7, p. 255; no enrolment traced; for abbreviated LP, see Ashmole MS 838, pp. 103–4.

1665 16 Mar.

CRAVEN, E.; Craven, V.
William Lord Craven.
Remainder (for earldom and viscountcy) to heirs male; extension of remainder of barony (1627) to William Craven, son and heir of Sir William Craven, Kt. deceased, and heirs male; failing whom to Sir Anthony Craven, Kt., brother of Sir William Craven and heirs male.
    C 231/7, p. 256; no enrolment traced; for LP, see E 403/2463, ff. 112–14v.

1665 16 Mar.

FRESCHEVILLE, B.
John Frescheville.
    C 231/7, p. 256; no enrolment traced; for abbreviated LP, see Ashmole MS 838, p. 108.

1665 17 Mar.   **FALMOUTH, E.**; Botetourt, B.
Charles Viscount Fitzhardinge (I).
C 231/7, p. 256; no enrolment traced; for abbreviated
LP, see Ashmole MS 838, pp. 109–10; dated 17 Mar. 1664
(*sic*) in *CP*, v, 246, 408.

1665 18 Mar.   **AILESBURY, E.**; Bruce, V.; Bruce, B.
Robert Earl of Elgin (S) and Lord Bruce (E).
C 231/7, p. 256; no enrolment traced; for LP, see E
403/2527, ff. 87v–90; dated 18 Mar. 1664 (*sic*) in *CP*, i,
58 but 18 Mar. 1665 in *ibid*. v, 42.

1665 20 Mar.   **BURLINGTON, E.**
Richard Earl of Cork (I) and Lord Clifford (E).
C 231/7, p. 257; no enrolment traced; for LP, see
E 403/2463, ff. 98v–99v; dated 20 Mar. 1664 (*sic*) in *CP*,
ii, 430 and *ibid*., iii, 421.

1665 23 Mar.   **ARUNDELL, B.**
Richard Arundell.
C 231/7, p. 257; no enrolment traced; for abbreviated
LP, see Ashmole MS 838, pp. 113–14; dated 23 Mar. 1664
(*sic*) in *CP*, ɪ, 262.

1665 11 Dec.   **CRAVEN, B.**
William Earl of Craven.
Remainder to barony of Craven (1627) confirmed to
Sir Anthony Craven, Bart. and heirs male failing whom
extended to Sir William Craven, Kt., son of Thomas
Craven, brother of Sir Anthony and heirs male.
C 231/7, p. 273; LP 17 Chas. II enrolled PR 18 Chas.
II, pt. 1 (C 66/3081) no. 7; dated 11 Dec. 1666 (*sic*) in
CP, iii, 501.

1667 7 Oct.   **CAMBRIDGE, D.**; Cambridge, E.; Dauntsey, B.
Edgar, son of James Duke of York.
C 231/7, p. 313; no enrolment traced; for LP, see
E 403/2527, ff. 19v–22.

1668 13 Jan.   **HALIFAX, V.**; Savile, B.
Sir George Savile, Bart.
C 231/7, p. 318; 19 Chas. II, pt. 2 (C 66/3091)
no. 14.

1669 27 Mar.   **HOWARD, B.**
Lord Henry Howard.
C 231/7, p. 342; no enrolment traced; for privy seal
warrant 22 Mar. 1669, *see* C 82/2385.

1670 3 Aug.   **CLEVELAND, D.**; Southampton, E; Nonsuch, B.
Barbara Countess of Castlemaine.
For life with remainder to Charles Lord Limerick her
eldest son (to be known as Earl of Southampton during
the life of his mother) and heirs male; failing whom to
George her second son and heirs male.
C 231/7, p. 375; no enrolment traced; for privy seal
warrant 29 July 1670, see Ashmole MS 838, pp. 113
bis–126.

1672 22 Apr.   **ARLINGTON, E.**; Thetford, V.; Arlington, B.
Henry Lord Arlington.
Remainder to heirs of body; failing whom, to brother,
Sir John Bennet, Kt. and heirs male.
C 231/7, p. 413; 24 Chas. II, pt. 2 (C 66/3135) no. 16.

1672 22 Apr.   **CLIFFORD, B.**
Sir Thomas Clifford, Kt.
C 231/7, p. 413; 24 Chas. II, pt. 2 (C 66/3135) no. 15.

1672 23 Apr.   **SHAFTESBURY, E.**; Cooper, B.
Anthony Lord Ashley.
C 231/7, p. 414; 24 Chas. II, pt. 2 (C 66/3135) no. 14.

1672 16 Aug.   **EUSTON, E.**; Ipswich, V.; Sudbury, B.
Henry FitzRoy.
Remainder, failing heirs male, to Lord George Fitzroy,
formerly Lord George Palmer, and heirs male.
C 231/7, p. 421; 24 Chas. II, pt. 2 (C 66/3135) no. 13.

1672 19 Oct.   **NORWICH, E.**
Henry Lord Howard.
Also grant of office of earl marshal with reversions.
C 231/7, p. 423; 24 Chas. II, pt. 10 (C 66/3142)
no. 36.

1673 29 Jan.   **DURAS, B.**
Lewis Marquess of Blanquefort.
C 231/7, p. 435; no enrolment traced; for privy seal
warrant 28 Jan. 1673, see Ashmole MS 838, pp. 159–61.

1673 15 Aug.
LATIMER, V.; Kiveton, B.
Thomas Viscount Osborne (S).
C 231/7, p. 458; 25 Chas. II, pt. 5 (C 66/3152) no. 5.

1673 19 Aug.
PORTSMOUTH, D.; Fareham, E.; Petersfield, B.
Louise de Keroualle.
For life.
C 231/7, p. 459; 25 Chas. II, pt. 10 (C 66/3152) no. 4.

1673 19 Aug.
YARMOUTH, V.; Paston, B.
Sir Robert Paston, Bart.
C 231/7, p. 459; 25 Chas. II, pt. 10 (C 66/3152) no. 2.

1673 27 Aug.
BUTLER, B.
Richard Earl of Arran (I).
C 231/7, p. 459; 25 Chas. II, pt. 10 (C 66/3152) no. 3.

1674 10 Jan.
FINCH, B.
Sir Heneage Finch, Bart.
C 231/7, p. 468; 25 Chas. II, pt. 1 (C 66/3143) no. 6.

1674 17 Mar.
BAYNING, V.
Anne Murray.
For life.
C 231/7, p. 474; 26 Chas. II, pt. 6 (C 66/3161) no. 11.

1674 1 Apr.
BELASYSE, B.
Lady Susan Belasyse.
For life.
C 231/7, p. 475; 26 Chas. II, pt. 5 (C 66/3160) no. 3.

1674 4 Apr.
POWIS, E.
William Lord Powis.
C 231/7, p. 476; 26 Chas. II, pt. 5 (C 66/3160) no. 2.

1674 5 June
LICHFIELD, E.; Quarendon, V.; Spelsbury, B.
Sir Edward Henry Lee, Bart.
C 231/7, p. 482; 26 Chas. II, pt. 5 (C 66/3160) no. 1.

1674 25 June
GUILFORD, E.; Petersham, B.
John Duke of Lauderdale (S).
C 231/7, p. 482; 26 Chas. II, pt. 5 (C 66/3160) no. 40.

1674 27 June

DANBY, E.
Thomas Viscount Latimer.
C 231/7, p. 478; 26 Chas. II, pt. 6 (C 66/3161) no. 10.

1674 1 Oct.

NORTHUMBERLAND, E.; Falmouth, V.;
Pontefract, B.
Lord George FitzRoy.
C 231/7, p. 485; 26 Chas. II, pt. 7 (C 66/3162) no. 5.

1674 5 Oct.

SUSSEX, E.
Thomas Lord Dacre.
C 231/7, p. 485; 26 Chas. II, pt. 7 (C 66/3162) no. 3.

1675 4 Feb.

MIDDLESEX, E.; Cranfield, B.
Charles Sackville *styled* Lord Buckhurst, eldest son of
Richard Earl of Dorset.
C 231/7, p. 492; 27 Chas. II, pt. 5 (C 66/3172) no. 21;
dated 4 Apr. (*sic*) in *CP*, viii, 692.

1675 11 Mar.

NEWPORT, V.
Francis Lord Newport.
C 231/7, p. 491; 27 Chas. II, pt. 5 (C 66/3172)
no. 29.

1675 29 July

PLYMOUTH, E.; Totnes, V.; Dartmouth, B.
Charles FitzCharles.
C 231/7, p. 500; 27 Chas. II, pt. 3 (C 66/3170)
no. 21.

1675 9 Aug.

RICHMOND, D.; March, E.; Settrington, B.
Charles Lennox.
C 231/7, p. 500; 27 Chas. II, pt. 3 (C 66/3170)
no. 32.

1675 10 Sept.

SOUTHAMPTON, D.; Chichester, E.; Newbury, B.
Charles FitzRoy *styled* Earl of Southampton, eldest son
of Barbara Duchess of Cleveland.
C 231/7, p. 502; no enrolment traced; for warrant
7 Sept. 1675, *see* C 82/2470.

1675 11 Sept.

GRAFTON, D.
Henry Earl of Euston.
C 231/7, p. 502; no enrolment traced; for warrant
7 Sept. 1675, *see* C 82/2470.

1676 8 Apr. **FEVERSHAM, E.**; Sondes, V.; Throwley, B.
Sir George Sondes, Kt.
For life with remainder to Lewis Lord Duras and heirs male.
C 231/7, p. 511; no enrolment traced.

1676 27 Dec. **BURFORD, E.**; Heddington, B.
Charles Beauclerk.
Remainder, failing heirs male, to brother James Beauclerk and heirs male.
C 231/7, p. 520; 28 Chas. II, pt. 3 (C 66/3182) no. 15.

1679 16 July **HALIFAX, E.**
George Viscount Halifax.
C 231/8, p. 10; 31 Chas. II, pt. 7 (C 66/3214) no. 3.

1679 21 July **MACCLESFIELD, E.**; Brandon, V.
Charles Lord Gerard.
C 231/8, p. 12; 31 Chas. II, pt. 7 (C 66/3214) no. 2.

1679 23 July **RADNOR, E.**; Bodmin, V.
John Lord Robartes.
C 231/8, p. 12; 31 Chas. II, pt. 5 (C 66/3212) no. 16.

1679 30 July **YARMOUTH, E.**
Robert Viscount Yarmouth.
C 231/8, p. 13; 31 Chas. II, pt. 5 (C 66/3214) no. 1.

1679 11 Sept. **BERKELEY, E.**; Dursley, V.
George Lord Berkeley.
C 231/8, p. 13; no enrolment traced; for original LP see M. F. Bond, *Guide to the Records of Parliament* (1971), 164.

1679 23 Oct. **CORBET, V.**
Sarah Corbet.
For life.
C 231/8, p. 15; no enrolment traced; for warrant, *see* C 82/2522.

1679 3 Dec. **CONWAY, E.**
Edward Viscount Conway.
C 231/8, p. 17; no enrolment traced.

1680 6 Sept. **SHEPPEY, E.**
Elizabeth Lady Dacre.
For life.
C 231/8, p. 36; 32 Chas. II, pt. 1 (C 66/3216) no. 7.

1681 3 Feb. **NOEL, B.**
Hon. Edward Noel.
C 231/8, p. 42; 33 Chas. II, pt. 2 (C 66/3220) no. 2;
CP, v, 599 states in error that remainder extended to
brothers, Hon. Baptist Noel and Hon. John Noel.

1681 23 Apr. **HYDE, V.**; Hyde, B.
Hon. Laurence Hyde.
C 231/8, p. 46; 33 Chas. II, pt. 3 (C 66/3221) no. 21.

1681 12 May **NOTTINGHAM, E.**
Heneage Lord Finch.
C 231/8, p. 47; 33 Chas. II, pt. 6 (C 66/3224) no. 13.

1681 31 May **LUMLEY, B.**
Richard Viscount Lumley (I).
Remainder, failing heirs male, to brother Henry
Lumley and heirs male.
C 231/8, p. 48; 33 Chas. II, pt. 6 (C 66/3224) no. 3.

1681 19 Oct. **CARTERET, B.**
Sir George Carteret, Bart.
Remainder, failing heirs male, to brothers Philip
Carteret and Edward Carteret and heirs male respectively.
C 231/8, p. 57; 33 Chas. II, pt. 6 (C 66/3224) no. 3.

1682 17 Aug. **HALIFAX, M.**
George Earl of Halifax.
C 231/8, p. 70; 34 Chas. II, pt. 6 (C 66/3231) no. 9;
dated 22 (*sic*) Aug. in *CP*, vi, 243.

1682 9 Nov. **ORMOND, D.**
James Duke of Ormond (I) and Earl of Brecknock (E).
C 231/8, p. 72; 34 Chas. II, pt. 8 (C 66/3233) no. 16.

1682 24 Nov. **OSSULSTON, B.**
Sir John Bennet, Kt.
C 231/8, p. 73; 34 Chas. II, pt. 8 (C 66/3233) no. 9.

1682 29 Nov.
ROCHESTER, E.
Laurence Viscount Hyde.
C 231/8, p. 73; 34 Chas. II, pt. 8 (C 66/3233) no. 8.

1682 30 Nov.
ABINGDON, E.
James Lord Norreys.
C 231/8, p. 73; 34 Chas. II, pt. 8 (C 66/3233) no. 6.

1682 1 Dec.
GAINSBOROUGH, E.
Edward Viscount Campden.
Remainder, failing heirs male, to brothers Hon. Baptist Noel and Hon. John Noel and heirs male respectively.
C 231/8, p. 74; 34 Chas. II, pt. 9 (C 66/3234) no. 29.

1682 2 Dec.
BEAUFORT, D.
Henry Marquess of Worcester.
C 231/8, p. 73; 34 Chas. II, pt. 9 (C 66/3234) no. 27.

1682 2 Dec.
TOWNSHEND, V.
Horatio Lord Townshend.
C 231/8, p. 73; 34 Chas. II, pt. 9 (C 66/3234) no. 26.

1682 2 Dec.
DARTMOUTH, B.
George Legge.
Remainder, failing heirs male, to William Legge and heirs male.
C 231/8, p. 73; 34 Chas. II, pt. 9 (C 66/3234) no. 25.

1682 5 Dec.
ALINGTON, B.
William Lord Alington (I).
C 231/8, p. 74; 34 Chas. II, pt. 9 (C 66/3234) no. 23.

1682 5 Dec.
HOLDERNESSE, E.
Conyers Lord Darcy.
C 231/8, p. 74; 34 Chas. II, pt. 9 (C 66/3234) no. 24.

1682 6 Dec.
PLYMOUTH, E.
Thomas Lord Windsor.
C 231/8, p. 73; 34 Chas. II, pt. 9 (C 66/3234) no. 22.

1682 11 Dec.
WEYMOUTH, V.; Thynne, B.
Sir Thomas Thynne, Bart.
Remainder, failing heirs male, to brothers James Thynne and Henry Frederick Thynne and heirs male respectively.
C 231/8, p. 74; 34 Chas. II, pt. 9 (C 66/3234) no. 21.

1683 15 Jan.   **STAWELL, B.**
Ralph Stawell.
C 231/8, p. 77; 34 Chas. II, pt. 9 (C 66/3234) no. 10.

1683 17 Jan.   **HATTON, V.**
Christopher Lord Hatton.
C 231/8, p. 80; 34 Chas. II, pt. 9 (C 66/3234) no. 6.

1683 6 Apr.   **NORTHUMBERLAND, D.**
George Earl of Northumberland.
C 231/8, p. 82; 35 Chas. II, pt. 1 (C 66/3235) no. 20.

1683 27 Sept.   **GUILFORD, B.**
Sir Francis North, Kt.
C 231/8, p. 89; 35 Chas. II, pt. 2 (C 66/3236) no. 48.

1684 10 Jan.   **ST. ALBANS, D.**
Charles Earl of Burford.
C 231/8, p. 95; 35 Chas. II, pt. 2 (C 66/3236) no. 52.

1684 8 Sept.   **GODOLPHIN, B.**
Sidney Godolphin.
C 231/8, p. 107; 36 Chas. II, pt. 5 (C 66/3245) no. 8;
dated 28 (*sic*) Sept. in *CP*, v, 747.

James II

1685 13 May   **DOVER, B.**
Henry Jermyn.
C 231/8, p. 128; 1 Jas. II, pt. 1 (C 66/3262) no. 38.

1685 14 May   **CHURCHILL, B.**
John Lord Churchill (S).
C 231/8, p. 129; 1 Jas. II, pt. 1 (C 66/3262) no. 39.

1685 15 May   **JEFFREYS, B.**
Sir George Jeffreys, Bart.
Remainder to heirs male by present wife Anne; failing whom to heirs male generally.
C 231/8, p. 129; 1 Jas. II, pt. 1 (C 66/3262) no. 37.

1686 20 Jan. **DORCHESTER, E.**; Darlington, B.
Katherine Sedley.
For life.
C 231/8, p. 143; 1 Jas. II, pt. 11 (C 66/3272) no. 14.

1686 20 Jan. **WALDEGRAVE, B.**
Sir Henry Waldegrave, Bart.
C 231/8, p. 143; 1 Jas. II, pt. 11 (C 66/3272) no. 13.

1687 19 Mar. **BERWICK, D.**; Tynemouth, E.; Bosworth, B.
James Fitzjames.
C 231/8, p. 176; 3 Jas. II, pt. 3 (C 66/3293) no. 29.

1687 24 Mar. **POWIS, M.**; Montgomery, V.
William Earl of Powis.
C 231/8, p. 172; 3 Jas. II, pt. 3 (C 66/3293) no. 25.

1688 7 Mar. **DERWENTWATER, E.**; Radclyffe, V.; Tyndale, B.
Sir Francis Radclyffe, Bart.
C 231/8, p. 189; 4 Jas. II, pt. 1 (C 66/3301) no. 11.

1688 5 Oct. **STAFFORD, E.**
Henry eldest son of late Viscount Stafford.
Remainder, failing heirs male, to John Howard and
Francis Howard, younger sons of said late Viscount and
heirs male respectively; rank of Countess granted to Mary
widow of same.
C 231/8, p. 200; 4 Jas. II, pt. 11 (C 66/3311) no. 15.

1688 3 Dec. **GRIFFIN, B.**
Edward Griffin.
C 231/8, p. 204 where dated 30 Nov. (*sic*); 4 Jas. II,
pt. 11 (C 66/3311) no. 14 where dated 3 Nov. (*sic*); it
seems probable that the latter is an error for 3 Dec., the
date assigned in *Lords Journals,* xiv, 108a and in *CP,* vi,
203.

William III and Mary II

1689 6 Apr. **CUMBERLAND, D.**; Kendal, E.; Ockingham, B.
Prince George.
C 231/8, p. 213; 1 Will. & Mar., pt. 2 (C 66/3326)
no. 15.

1689 8 Apr.

BOLTON, D.
Charles Marquess of Winchester.
C 231/8, p. 213; 1 Will. & Mar., pt. 2 (C 66/3326) no. 14; dated 9 (*sic*) Apr. in *CP*, ii, 210 but 8 Apr. in *ibid.*, xii, pt. 2, 769.

1689 9 Apr.

FAUCONBERG, E.
Thomas Viscount Fauconberg.
C 231/8, p. 213; 1 Will. & Mar., pt. 2 (C 66/3326) no. 12.

1689 9 Apr.

MONMOUTH, E.
Charles Viscount Mordaunt.
C 231/8, p. 213; 1 Will. & Mar., pt. 2 (C 66/3326) no. 11.

1689 9 Apr.

MARLBOROUGH, E.
John Lord Churchill (S & E).
C 231/8, p. 213; 1 Will. & Mar., pt. 2 (C 66/3326) no. 9.

1689 9 Apr.

MONTAGU, E.; Monthermer, V.
Ralph Lord Montagu.
C 231/8, p. 214; 1 Will. & Mar., pt. 2 (C 66/3326) no. 10.

1689 9 Apr.

SYDNEY, V.; Milton, B.
Henry Sydney.
C 231/8, p. 214; 1 Will. & Mar., pt. 2 (C 66/3326) no. 8.

1689 9 Apr.

PORTLAND, E.; Woodstock, V.; Cirencester, B.
William Bentinck.
C 231/8, p. 214; 1 Will. & Mar., pt. 2 (C 66/3326) no. 13.

1689 9 Apr.

CHOLMONDELEY, B.
Hugh Viscount Cholmondeley (I).
C 231/8, p. 214; 1 Will. & Mar., pt. 2 (C 66/3326) no. 6; dated 10 Apr. (*sic*) in *CP*, iii, 201 where it is stated in error that remainder extended to brother, Hon. George Cholmondeley.

1689 10 Apr.   **LUMLEY, V.**
Richard Viscount Lumley (I) and Lord Lumley (E).
C 231/8, p. 214; 1 Will. & Mar., pt. 2 (C 66/3326) no. 7;
dated 9 (*sic*) Apr. in *CP*, viii, 281 but 10 Apr. in *ibid.*, xi, 509.

1689 20 Apr.   **CARMARTHEN, M.**
Thomas Earl of Danby.
C 231/8, p. 217; 1 Will. & Mar., pt. 2 (C 66/3326)
no. 4.

1689 9 May   **SCHOMBERG, D.**; Harwich, M.; Brentford, E.; Teyes, B.
Frederick Schomberg.
For life with remainder to third son Charles
Schomberg and heirs male; failing whom to second son
Meinhard Schomberg and heirs male; failing whom to
heirs male.
C 231/8, p. 227; 1 Will. & Mar., pt. 2 (C 66/3326)
no. 3.

1689 29 May   **TORRINGTON, E.**; Herbert, B.
Arthur Herbert.
Remainder (for earldom) to heirs male; (for barony) to
same; failing whom, to brother Charles Herbert and heirs
male.
C 231/8, p. 226; 1 Will. & Mar., pt. 2 (C 66/3326) no. 2;
CP, xii, pt. 1, 786 states in error that special remainder
applied to both earldom and barony.

1689 30 May   **ASHBURNHAM, B.**
John Ashburnham.
C 231/8, p. 226; 1 Will. & Mar., pt. 2 (C 66/3326)
no. 1; dated 20 (*sic*) May in *CP*, i, 271.

1690 15 Apr.   **SCARBROUGH, E.**
Richard Viscount Lumley (I & E).
C 231/8, p. 254; 2 Will. & Mar., pt. 1 (C 66/3334)
no. 10.

1690 17 Apr.   **WARRINGTON, E.**
Henry Lord Delamer.
C 231/8, p. 255; 2 Will. & Mar., pt. 1 (C 66/3334)
no. 8.

1690 21 Apr.   **LONGUEVILLE, V.**
Henry Lord Grey.
Remainder, failing heirs male, to brother Hon.
Christopher Yelverton and heirs male.
C 231/8, p. 255; 2 Will. & Mar., pt. 1 (C 66/3334) no.
7; *CP*, vi, 162 omits mention of remainder to Yelverton.

1691 20 Mar.   **VILLIERS, V.**; Villiers, B.
Sir Edward Villiers, Kt.
C 231/8, p. 269; 3 Will. & Mar., pt. 1 (C 66/3340)
no. 5.

1692 11 Apr.   **CAPELL, B.**
Sir Henry Capell, Kt.
C 231/8, p. 287; 4 Will. & Mar., pt. 3 (C 66/3351)
no. 13.

1692 12 Apr.   **LEOMINSTER, B.**
Sir William Fermor, Bart.
C 231/8, p. 287; 4 Will. & Mar., pt. 3 (C 66/3351)
no. 12.

1694 23 Jan.   **BUTLER, B.**
Hon. Charles Butler.
C 231/8, p. 314; 5 Will. & Mar., pt. 2 (C 66/3360)
no. 5.

1694 28 Apr.   **HERBERT, B.**
Henry Herbert.
C 231/8, p. 319; 6 Will. & Mar., pt. 7 (C 66/3372)
no. 10.

1694 30 Apr.   **SHREWSBURY, D.**; Alton, M.
Charles Earl of Shrewsbury.
C 231/8, p. 319; 6 Will. & Mar., pt. 7 (C 66/3372)
no. 9.

1694 4 May   **LEEDS, D.**
Thomas Marquess of Carmarthen.
C 231/8, p. 319; 6 Will. & Mar., pt. 3 (C 66/3369)
no. 17.

1694 10 May   **NORMANBY, M.**
John Earl of Mulgrave.
C 231/8, p. 321; 6 Will. & Mar., pt. 7 (C 66/3372)
no. 8.

1694 11 May   **BRADFORD, E.**
                    Francis Viscount Newport.
                    C 231/8, p. 320; 6 Will. & Mar., pt. 7 (C 66/3372)
                    no. 7.

1694 11 May   **BEDFORD, D.**; Tavistock, M.
                    William Earl of Bedford.
                    For life with remainder to Wriothesley Russell and
                    heirs male; failing whom to heirs male.
                    C 231/8, p. 321; 6 Will. & Mar., pt. 3 (C 66/3369)
                    no. 9.

1694 12 May   **DEVONSHIRE, D.**; Hartington, M.
                    William Earl of Devonshire.
                    C 231/8, p. 321; 6 Will. & Mar., pt. 3 (C 66/3369)
                    no. 8.

1694 14 May   **ROMNEY, E.**
                    Henry Viscount Sydney.
                    C 231/8, p. 320; 6 Will. & Mar., pt. 3 (C 66/3369)
                    no. 7.

1694 14 May   **NEWCASTLE UPON TYNE, D.**; Clare, M.
                    John Earl of Clare.
                    C 231/8, p. 322; 6 Will. & Mar., pt. 3 (C 66/3369)
                    no. 6.

William III

1695 10 May   **ROCHFORD, E.**; Tunbridge, V.; Enfield, B.
                    William Nassau de Zuylestein.
                    C 231/8, p. 340; 7 Will. III, pt. 1 (C 66/3378) no. 24.

1695 11 May   **TANKERVILLE, E.**; Glendale, V.
                    Ford Lord Grey.
                    C 231/8, p. 337 where dated 11 June (*sic*); 7 Will. III,
                    pt. 1 (C 66/3378) no. 22 where dated 11 May (*sic*); the
                    latter has been preferred since the entry in the docket
                    book is, exceptionally, out of sequence and the
                    authorizing warrant is dated 3 May as is that for
                    Rochford (above) (*Calendar of State Papers Domestic
                    1694–5*, p. 453); dated 11 June (*sic*) in *CP*, viii, 170 and
                    ibid., xii, pt. 1, 632.

1695 13 May   **HOWLAND, B.**
                       William Duke of Bedford.
                       For life with remainder to grandson Wriothesley
                       Russell *styled* Marquess of Tavistock and heirs male by
                       Elizabeth Howland.
                           C 231/8, p. 338 where dated 13 June (*sic*); 7 Will. III,
                       pt. 1 (C 66/3378) no. 21 where dated 13 May (*sic*); the
                       latter has been preferred since the entry in the docket
                       book is, exceptionally, out of sequence and the author-
                       izing warrant is dated 2 May (*Calendar of State Papers
                       Domestic 1694–5,* p. 452); original LP dated 13 May
                       (information kindly supplied by Mrs. A. Mitchell,
                       Archivist, Woburn Abbey); dated 13 June (*sic*) in *CP,* ii,
                       79.

1696 4 May   **HAVERSHAM, B.**
                       Sir John Thompson, Bart.
                           C 231/8, p. 352; 8 Will. III, pt. 5 (C 66/3386) no. 8.

1696 28 May   **LONSDALE, V.**; Lowther, B.
                       Sir John Lowther, Bart.
                           C 231/8, p. 353; 8 Will. III, pt. 8 (C 66/3389) no. 8.

1697 10 Feb.   **ALBEMARLE, E.**; Bury, V.; Ashford, B.
                       Arnold Joost de Keppel.
                           C 231/8, p. 363; 8 Will. III, pt. 3 (C 66/3382) no. 2.

1697 26 Apr.   **COVENTRY, E.**; Deerhurst, V.
                       Thomas Lord Coventry.
                           Remainder, failing heirs male, to Francis Coventry
                       younger son of Thomas late Lord Coventry; William
                       Coventry son of Walter Coventry younger brother of said
                       Thomas Lord Coventry; and Thomas Coventry and
                       Henry Coventry brothers of said William Coventry and
                       heirs male respectively.
                           C 231/8, p. 367; 9 Will. III, pt. 2 (C 66/3391) no. 8.

1697 7 May   **ORFORD, E.**; Barfleur, V.; Shingay, B.
                       Edward Russell.
                           Remainder (for earldom and viscountcy) to heirs male;
                       (for barony) to same, failing whom, to Edward Cheeke of
                       Pirgo, Essex, and heirs male.
                           C 231/8, p. 368; 9 Will. III, pt. 1 (C 66/3390) no. 11.

1697 24 Sept.   **JERSEY, E.**
Edward Viscount Villiers.
C 231/8, p. 377; no enrolment traced; dated 13 Oct.
(*sic*) in *CP*, vii, 88.

1697 2 Dec.   **SOMERS, B.**
Sir John Somers, Kt.
C 231/8, p. 382; 9 Will. III, pt. 5 (C 66/3394) no. 12.

1698 25 July   **BARNARD, B.**
Christopher Vane.
C 231/8, p. 392; 10 Will. III, pt. 5 (C 66/3402)
no. 13.

1698 24 Dec.   **GRANTHAM, E.**; Boston, V.; Alford, B.
Henry d'Auverquerque the younger, son of Henry
d'Auverquerque the elder.
Remainder, failing heirs male, to Cornelius, Maurice
and Francis, second, third and fourth sons of Henry
d'Auverquerque the elder and their heirs male
respectively.
C 231/8, p. 401; 10 Will. III, pt. 1 (C 66/3398)
no. 10.

1700 13 Dec.   **HALIFAX, B.**
Charles Montagu.
Remainder failing heirs male to nephew George
Montagu and heirs male.
C 231/9, p. 17; 12 Will. III, pt. 1 (C 66/3414) no. 2.

Anne

1702 14 Dec.   **MARLBOROUGH, D.**; Blandford, M.
John Earl of Marlborough.
C 231/9, p. 84; 1 Ann., pt. 14 (C 66/3437) no. 13.

1703 13 Mar.   **GRANVILLE, B.**
Hon. John Granville.
C 231/9, p. 91; 2 Ann., pt. 2 (C 66/3439) no. 25.

1703 15 Mar.   **GUERNSEY, B.**
Hon. Heneage Finch.
C 231/9, p. 91; 2 Ann., pt. 2 (C 66/3439) no. 26.

1703 16 Mar.   **GOWER, B.**
                      Sir John Leveson Gower, Bart.
                      C 231/9, p. 91; 2 Ann., pt. 2 (C 66/3439) no. 27.

1703 17 Mar.   **CONWAY, B.**
                      Francis Seymour Conway.
                      Remainder, failing heirs male, to brother Charles
                      Seymour and heirs male.
                      C 231/9, p. 92; 2 Ann., pt. 2 (C 66/3439) no. 22;
                      CP, iii, 402 omits mention of remainder to Seymour.

1703 23 Mar.   **HERVEY, B.**
                      John Hervey.
                      C 231/9, p. 92; 2 Ann., pt. 2 (C 66/3439) no. 12.

1703 24 Mar.   **BUCKINGHAM & NORMANBY, D.**
                      John Marquess of Normanby.
                      C 231/9, p. 92; 2 Ann., pt. 2 (C 66/3439) no. 20;
                      dated 23 (*sic*) Mar. in *CP*, ii, 398 but 24 Mar. in *ibid.*,
                      ix, 638.

1703 29 Mar.   **RUTLAND, D.**; Granby, M.
                      John Earl of Rutland.
                      C 231/9, p. 93; 2 Ann., pt. 2 (C 66/3439) no. 17.

1705 14 Apr.   **MONTAGU, D.**; Monthermer, M.
                      Ralph Earl of Montagu.
                      C 231/9, p. 124; 4 Ann., pt. 1 (C 66/3448) no. 16.

1705 26 Nov.   **GREENWICH, E.**; Chatham, B.
                      John Duke of Argyll (S).
                      C 231/9, p. 134; 4 Ann., pt. 4 (C 66/3451) no. 9.

1706 9 Dec.   **CAMBRIDGE, D.**; Cambridge, M.; Milford
                      Haven, E.; Northallerton, V.; Tewkesbury, B.
                      Prince George Lewis.
                      C 231/9, p. 147; 5 Ann., pt. 2 (C 66/3454) no. 3;
                      dated 9 Nov. (*sic*) in *CP*, ii, 497.

1706 14 Dec.   **KENT, M.**; Harold, E.; Goderich, V.
                      Henry Earl of Kent.
                      C 231/9, p. 148; 5 Ann., pt. 2 (C 66/3454) no. 1;
                      dated 14 Nov. (*sic*) in *CP* , vii, 177.

1706 14 Dec.   **COWPER, B.**
                 Sir William Cowper, Bart.
                 C 231/9, p. 147; 5 Ann., pt. 2 (C 66/3454) no. 17.

1706 16 Dec.   **PELHAM, B.**
                 Sir Thomas Pelham, Bart.
                 C 231/9, p. 147; 5 Ann., pt. 2 (C 66/3454) no. 4.

1706 21 Dec.   **LINDSEY, M.**
                 Robert Earl of Lindsey.
                 Remainder, failing heirs male, to heirs male of late
                 father Robert Earl of Lindsey by wife Elizabeth Wharton.
                 C 231/9, p. 148; 5 Ann., pt. 1 (C 66/3453) no. 38.

1706 23 Dec.   **DORCHESTER, M.**
                 Evelyn Earl of Kingston.
                 Remainder, failing heirs male, to uncle Gervase Lord
                 Pierrepont (I) and heirs male.
                 C 231/9, p. 148; 5 Ann., pt. 1 (C 66/3453) no. 37.

1706 23 Dec.   **WHARTON, E.**; Winchendon, V.
                 Thomas Lord Wharton.
                 C 231/9, p. 149; 5 Ann., pt. 1 (C 66/3453) no. 35.

1706 24 Dec.   **POULETT, E.**; Hinton, V.
                 John Lord Poulett.
                 C 231/9, p. 149; 5 Ann., pt. 1 (C 66/3453) no. 36.

1706 26 Dec.   **GODOLPHIN, E.**; Rialton, V.
                 Sidney Lord Godolphin.
                 C 231/9, p. 149; 5 Ann., pt. 1 (C 66/3453) no. 34.

1706 27 Dec.   **CHOLMONDELEY, E.**; Malpas, V.
                 Hugh Viscount Cholmondeley (I) and Lord
                 Cholmondeley (E).
                 Remainder, failing heirs male, to Hon. George
                 Cholmondeley and heirs male.
                 C 231/9, p. 149; 5 Ann., pt. 1 (C 66/3453) no. 33;
                 dated 29 (*sic*) Dec. in *CP*, iii, 201.

1706 30 Dec.   **BINDON, E.**; Chesterford, B.
                 Henry Howard *styled* Lord Walden, eldest son of
                 Henry Earl of Suffolk.
                 C 231/9, p. 149; 5 Ann., pt. 1 (C 66/3453) no. 32.

1708 26 May   **DOVER, D.**; Beverley, M.; Ripon, B.
James Duke of Queensberry (S).
For life with remainder to second son Charles Earl of Solway (S), third son Lord George Douglas, fourth, fifth and any other sons and heirs male respectively.
C 231/9, p. 174; 7 Ann., pt. 2 (C 66/3464) no. 8.

1710 28 Apr.   **KENT, D.**
Henry Marquess of Kent.
C 231/9, p. 203; 9 Ann., pt. 1 (C 66/3473) no. 8.

1711 23 May   **OXFORD & MORTIMER, E.**; Harley, B.
Robert Harley.
Remainder, failing heirs male, to heirs male of grandfather, Sir Robert Harley, Kt.
C 231/9, p. 231; 10 Ann., pt. 1 (C 66/3479) no. 24.

1711 3 Sept.   **FERRERS, E.**; Tamworth, V.
Robert Lord Ferrers.
C 231/9, p. 239; 10 Ann., pt. 6 (C 66/3484) no. 27.

1711 3 Sept.   **HARCOURT, B.**
Sir Simon Harcourt, Kt.
C 231/9, p. 239; 10 Ann., pt. 6 (C 66/3484) no. 28.

1711 4 Sept.   **STRAFFORD, E.**; Wentworth, V.
Thomas Lord Raby.
Remainder, failing heirs male, to brother Peter Wentworth and heirs male.
C 231/9, p. 239; 10 Ann., pt. 4 (C 66/3482) no. 1; dated 29 June (*sic*) in *CP*, xii, pt. 1, 330.

1711 5 Sept.   **DARTMOUTH, E.**; Lewisham, V.
William Lord Dartmouth.
C 231/9, p. 240; 10 Ann., pt. 6 (C 66/3484) no. 19.

1711 5 Sept.   **BOYLE, B.**
Charles Earl of Orrery (I).
C 231/9, p. 240; 10 Ann., pt. 6 (C 66/3484) no. 25.

1711 10 Sept.   **BRANDON, D.**; Dutton, B.
James Duke of Hamilton (S).
Remainder, failing heirs male, to heirs male of parents, William late Duke and Anne Duchess of Hamilton (S).
C 231/9, p. 240; 10 Ann., pt. 6 (C 66/3484) no. 18.

1711 31 Dec.

HAY, B.
Hon. George Hay.
C 231/9, p. 251; 10 Ann., pt. 3 (C 66/3481) no. 24.

1712 1 Jan.
7 a.m.

MOUNTJOY, B.
Thomas Viscount Windsor (I).
C 231/9, p. 251; 10 Ann., pt. 3 (C 66/3481) no. 23.

1712 1 Jan.
8 a.m.

BURTON, B.
Hon. Henry Paget.
C 231/9, p. 252; 10 Ann., pt. 3 (C 66/3481) no. 19.

1712 1 Jan.
9 a.m.

MANSELL, B.
Sir Thomas Mansell, Bart.
C 231/9, p. 252; 10 Ann., pt. 3 (C 66/3481) no. 18.

1712 1 Jan.
10 a.m.

MIDDLETON, B.
Sir Thomas Willoughby, Bart.
C 231/9, p. 252; 10 Ann., pt. 3 (C 66/3481) no. 17.

1712 1 Jan.
11 a.m.

TREVOR, B.
Sir Thomas Trevor, Kt.
C 231/9, p. 252; 10 Ann., pt. 3 (C 66/3481) no. 16.

1712 1 Jan.
1 p.m.

LANSDOWNE, B.
George Granville.
C 231/9, p. 252; 10 Ann., pt. 3 (C 66/3481) no. 15.

1712 1 Jan.
2 p.m.

MASHAM, B.
Samuel Masham.
C 231/9, p. 252; 10 Ann., pt. 3 (C 66/3481) no. 14.

1712 1 Jan.
3 p.m.

FOLEY, B.
Thomas Foley.
C 231/9, p. 252; 10 Ann., pt. 3 (C 66/3481) no. 13.

1712 1 Jan.
4 p.m.

BATHURST, B.
Allen Bathurst.
C 231/9, p. 253; 10 Ann., pt. 3 (C 66/3481) no. 12.

1712 7 July

BOLINGBROKE, V.; St. John, B.
Henry St. John.
Remainder, failing heirs male, to father Sir Henry St. John, Bart. and heirs male.
C 231/9, p. 264; 11 Ann., pt. 2 (C 66/3487) no. 6.

1713 21 July   **BINGLEY, B.**
                        Robert Benson.
                        C 231/9, p. 288; 12 Ann., pt. 4 (C 66/3492) no. 12.

George I

1714 27 Sept.   **WALES, P.**; Chester, E.
                        Prince George Augustus.
                        Remainder to heirs, kings of Great Britain.
                        C 231/9, p. 314; 1 Geo. I, pt. 1 (C 66/3498) no. 3.

1714 19 Oct.   **UXBRIDGE, E.**
                        Henry Lord Paget and Burton.
                        C 231/9, p. 317; 1 Geo. I, pt. 12 (C 66/3509) no. 18.

1714 19 Oct.   **CARNARVON, E.**; Wilton, V.
                        James Lord Chandos.
                        Remainder, failing heirs male, to brother Hon. Henry
                        Brydges and heirs male.
                        C 231/9, p. 317; 1 Geo. I, pt. 11 (C 66/3508) no. 17
                        where dated 9 (*sic*) Oct.

1714 19 Oct.   **ROCKINGHAM, E.**; Sondes, V.; Throwley, B.
                        Lewis Lord Rockingham.
                        C 231/9, p. 318; 1 Geo. I, pt. 11 (C 66/3508) no. 19
                        where dated 9 (*sic*) Oct.

1714 19 Oct.   **TANKERVILLE, E.**
                        Charles Lord Ossulston.
                        C 231/9, p. 318; 1 Geo. I, pt. 12 (C 66/3509) no. 25.

1714 19 Oct.   **HALIFAX, E.**; Sunbury, V.
                        Charles Lord Halifax.
                        C 231/9, p. 318; 1 Geo. I, pt. 12 (C 66/3509) no. 24.

1714 19 Oct.   **AYLESFORD, E.**
                        Heneage Lord Guernsey.
                        C 231/9, p. 318; 1 Geo. I, pt. 12 (C 66/3509) no. 19.

1714 19 Oct.   **BRISTOL, E.**
                        John Lord Hervey.
                        C 231/9, p. 318; 1 Geo. I, pt. 12 (C 66/3509) no. 20.

1714 19 Oct. **CLARE, E.**; Houghton, V.
     Thomas Holles Lord Pelham.
     Remainder, failing heirs male, to brother Hon. Henry
    Pelham and heirs male.
     C 231/9, p. 318; 1 Geo. I, pt. 13 (C 66/3510) no. 41.

1714 19 Oct. **TADCASTER, V.**
     Henry Earl of Thomond (I).
     C 231/9, p. 319; 1 Geo. I, pt. 12 (C 66/3509) no. 21.

1714 19 Oct. **SAUNDERSON, B.**
     James Viscount Castleton (I).
     C 231/9, p. 319; 1 Geo. I, pt. 12 (C 66/3509) no. 17.

1714 19 Oct. **PIERREPONT, B.**
     Gervase Lord Pierrepont (I).
     C 231/9, p. 319; 1 Geo. I, pt. 12 (C 66/3509) no. 22.

1714 19 Oct. **HARBOROUGH, B.**
     Bennet Lord Sherard (I).
     Remainder, failing heirs male, to Philip Sherard of
    Whissendine, Rutland and heirs male.
     C 231/9, p. 319; 1 Geo. I, pt. 12 (C 66/3509) no. 26.

1714 19 Oct. **CARLETON, B.**
     Hon. Henry Boyle.
     C 231/9, p. 319; 1 Geo. I, pt. 12 (C 66/3509) no. 23.

1714 19 Oct. **COBHAM, B.**
     Sir Richard Temple, Bart.
     C 231/9, p. 319; 1 Geo. I, pt. 12 (C 66/3509) no. 27.

1715 1 Jan. **GRANVILLE, E.**; Carteret, V.
     Grace Lady Carteret.
     Remainder (for earldom) to heirs male; (for
    viscountcy) to same, failing whom, to Edward Carteret,
    brother of George Lord Carteret, late husband of
    grantee and heirs male.
     C 231/9, p. 341; 1 Geo. I, pt. 6 (C 66/3503) no. 15.

1715 15 Feb. **WHARTON, M.**; Malmesbury, M.
     Thomas Earl of Wharton.
     C 231/9, p. 349; 1 Geo. I, pt. 6 (C 66/3503) no. 14.

1715 14 June   **HALIFAX, E.**; Sunbury, V.
                       George Lord Halifax.
                       C 231/9, p. 358; 1 Geo. I, pt. 10 (C 66/3507) no. 15.

1715 26 July   **ANCASTER & KESTEVEN, D.**
                       Robert Marquess of Lindsey.
                       Remainder, failing heirs male, to heirs male of father,
                       Robert late Earl of Lindsey by his wife, Elizabeth.
                       C 231/9, p. 362; 1 Geo. I, pt. 10 (C 66/3507) no. 14.

1715 10 Aug.   **KINGSTON UPON HULL, D.**
                       Evelyn Marquess of Dorchester.
                       C 231/9, p. 365; 2 Geo. I, pt. 2 (C 66/3512) no. 11.

1715 11 Aug.   **NEWCASTLE UPON TYNE, D.**; Clare, M.
                       Thomas Earl of Clare.
                       Remainder, failing heirs male, to brother Hon. Henry
                       Pelham and heirs male.
                       C 231/9, p. 366; 2 Geo. I, pt. 2 (C 66/3512) no. 19.

1716 10 Mar.   **PARKER, B.**
                       Sir Thomas Parker, Kt.
                       C 231/9, p. 383; 2 Geo. I, pt. 3 (C 66/3513) no. 28.

1716 18 June   **CONINGSBY, B.**
                       Thomas Lord Coningsby (I).
                       Remainder to issue male by any woman or women
                       whom he shall subsequently marry.
                       C 231/9, p. 395; 2 Geo. I, pt. 5 (C 66/3515) no. 17.

1716 19 June   **ONSLOW, B.**
                       Sir Richard Onslow, Bart.
                       Remainder, failing heirs male, to uncle Denzil
                       Onslow of Pyrford, Surrey, and heirs male; failing whom
                       to heirs male of father, Sir Arthur Onslow, Bart.
                       C 231/9, p. 395; 2 Geo. I, pt. 5 (C 66/3515) no. 18.

1716 20 June   **TORRINGTON, B.**
                       Thomas Newport.
                       C 231/9, p. 396; 2 Geo. I, pt. 5 (C 66/3515) no. 15.

1716 21 June   **CADOGAN, B.**
                       William Cadogan.
                       C 231/9, p. 396; 2 Geo. I, pt. 5 (C 66/3515) no. 30.

1716 22 June

ROMNEY, B.
Sir Robert Marsham, Bart.
C 231/9, p. 396; 2 Geo. I, pt. 5 (C 66/3515) no. 19.

1716 30 June

CASTLETON, V.
James Viscount Castleton (I) and Lord Saunderson
(GB).
C 231/9, p. 399; 2 Geo. I, pt. 5 (C 66/3515) no. 16;
dated 2 July (*sic*) in *CP*, iii, 101.

1716 2 July

ST. JOHN, V.; St. John, B.
Sir Henry St. John, Bart.
For life with remainder to second son, John St. John
and heirs male; failing whom to heirs male of said Sir
Henry hereafter to be begotten.
C 231/9, p. 399; 2 Geo. I, pt. 5 (C 66/3515) no. 14.

1716 5 July

YORK & ALBANY, D.; Ulster, E. (I)
Prince Ernest Augustus.
C 231/9, p. 400; 2 Geo. I, pt. 4 (C 66/3514) no. 15.

1716 6 July

PORTLAND, D.; Titchfield, M.
Henry Earl of Portland.
C 231/9, p. 401; 2 Geo. I, pt. 4 (C 66/3514) no. 16.

1716 10 July

NEWBURGH, B.
George Lord Newborough (I).
C 231/9, p. 401; 2 Geo. I, pt. 5 (C 66/3514) no. 25.

1717 26 Jan.

CONINGSBY, V.; Hampton Court, B.
Hon. Margaret Coningsby.
C 231/9, p. 413; 3 Geo. I, pt. 1 (C 66/3517) no. 1.

1717 13 July

STANHOPE, V.; Stanhope, B.
James Stanhope.
Remainder, failing heirs male, to heirs male of John
Stanhope, of Elvaston, Derbyshire.
C 231/9, p. 425; 3 Geo. I, pt. 4 (C 66/3520) no. 1;
dated 3 (*sic*) July in *CP*, xii, pt. 1, 232.

1717 26 Sept.

SUSSEX, E.
Talbot Viscount Longueville.
Remainder, failing heirs male, to brother Hon. Henry
Yelverton and heirs male.
C 231/9, p. 434; 4 Geo. I, pt. 2 (C 66/3522) no. 12.

1718 28 Jan.

WHARTON, D.
Philip Marquess of Wharton.
C 231/9, p. 441; 4 Geo. I, pt. 1 (C 66/3521) no. 12.

1718 20 Mar.

COWPER, E.; Fordwich, V.
William Lord Cowper.
Remainder, failing heirs male, to brother Spencer
Cowper and heirs male; extension of remainder of
barony of Cowper (1706) to said Spencer Cowper and
heirs male.
    C 231/9, p. 445; 4 Geo. I, pt. 3 (C 66/3523) no. 11;
dated 18 (*sic*) Mar. in *CP*, iii, 483.

1718 14 Apr.

STANHOPE, E.
James Viscount Stanhope.
C 231/9, p. 449; 4 Geo. I, pt. 3 (C 66/3523) no. 4.

1718 1 May

CADOGAN, E.; Caversham, V.; Cadogan, B.
William Lord Cadogan
Remainder (for earldom and viscountcy) to heirs
male; (for barony) failing heirs male, to brother Charles
Cadogan and heirs male.
    C 231/9, p. 450; 4 Geo. I, pt. 5 (C 66/3525) no. 11;
dated 8 (*sic*) May in *CP*, ii, 460.

1718 23 May

COBHAM, V.
Richard Lord Cobham.
    Remainder, failing heirs male, to second and third
sisters Hester Grenville and Christian Lyttelton and heirs
male respectively; extension of remainder of barony of
Cobham (1714) to said Hester Grenville and Christian
Lyttelton.
    C 231/9, p. 452; 4 Geo. I, pt. 7 (C 66/3527) no. 2;
CP, iii, 341 states in error that a second barony of
Cobham was created on this occasion.

1718 31 Oct.

SHERARD, V.
Bennet Lord Sherard (I) and Lord Harborough (GB).
C 231/9, p. 459; 5 Geo. I, pt. 2 (C 66/3529) no. 30.

1719 19 Mar.

KENDAL, D.; Feversham, E.; Glastonbury, B.
Ermengard Melusina Duchess of Munster (I).
For life.
C 231/9, p. 467; 5 Geo. I, pt. 3 (C 66/3530) no. 9.

1719 27 Apr.

GREENWICH, D.
John Duke of Argyll (S) and Earl of Greenwich (E).
C 231/9, p. 469; 5 Geo. I, pt. 3 (C 66/3530) no. 14.

1719 28 Apr.

MANCHESTER, D.
Charles Earl of Manchester.
C 231/9, p. 469; 5 Geo. I, pt. 3 (C 66/3530) no. 12.

1719 29 Apr.

CHANDOS, D.; Carnarvon, M.
James Earl of Carnarvon.
C 231/9, p. 470; 5 Geo. I, pt. 3 (C 66/3530) no. 10.

1719 8 May

HARBOROUGH, E.
Bennet Viscount Sherard.
Remainder, failing heirs male, to Philip Sherard of
Whissendine, Rutland, and heirs male.
C 231/9, p. 471; 5 Geo. I, pt. 3 (C 66/3530) no. 13.

1719 9 May

CONINGSBY, E.
Thomas Lord Coningsby.
Remainder to heirs male by any wife he shall
hereafter marry; failing whom to Margaret Viscountess
Coningsby, his elder daughter by Lady Frances, his
second wife; after whose death and failing issue of said
Thomas to heirs male of said Margaret.
C 231/9, p. 471; 5 Geo. I, pt. 3 (C 66/3530) no. 11;
dated 30 Apr. (*sic*) in *CP*, iii, 395, 397.

1720 9 June

DUCIE, B.
Matthew Ducie Moreton.
C 231/9, p. 495; 6 Geo. I, pt. 6 (C 66/3538) no. 4.

1720 9 June

FALMOUTH, V.; Boscawen Rose, B.
Hugh Boscawen.
C 231/9, p. 495; 6 Geo. I, pt. 7 (C 66/3539) no. 11.

1720 11 June

LYMINGTON, V.; Wallop, B.
John Wallop.
C 231/9, p. 496; 6 Geo. I, pt. 6 (C 66/3538) no. 6.

1720 17 June

DORSET, D.
Lionel Earl of Dorset & Middlesex.
C 231/9, p. 499; 6 Geo. I, pt. 6 (C 66/3538) no. 11.

1720 18 June

BRIDGWATER, D.; Brackley, M.
Scroop Earl of Bridgwater.
C 231/9, p. 500; 6 Geo. I, pt. 6 (C 66/3538) no. 9.

1720 18 June   **CASTLETON, E.**
James Viscount Castleton (I & GB).
C 231/9, p. 501; 6 Geo. I, pt. 6 (C 66/3538) no. 3.

1721 4 Sept.   **LECHMERE, B.**
Nicholas Lechmere.
C 231/10, p. 2; 8 Geo. I, pt. 1 (C 66/3545) no. 12.

1721 11 Sept.   **HARCOURT, V.**
Simon Lord Harcourt.
C 231/10, p. 2; 8 Geo. I, pt. 1 (C 66/3545) no. 3.

1721 21 Sept.   **TORRINGTON, V.**; Byng, B.
Sir George Byng, Bart.
C 231/10, p. 4; 8 Geo. I, pt. 1 (C 66/3545) no. 15.

1721 15 Nov.   **MACCLESFIELD, E.**; Parker, V.
Thomas Lord Parker.
Remainder, failing heirs male, to daughter Hon.
Elizabeth Heathcote and heirs male.
C 231/10, p. 7; 8 Geo. I, pt. 2 (C 66/3546) no. 40.

1721 27 Dec.   **POMFRET, E.**
Thomas Lord Leominster.
C 231/10, p. 12; 8 Geo. I, pt. 2 (C 66/3546) no. 21.

1722 6 Apr.   **DARLINGTON, E.**; Brentford, B.
Sophia Charlotte Countess of Leinster (I).
For life.
C 231/10, p. 20; 8 Geo. I, pt. 4 (C 66/3548) no. 21.

1722 7 Apr.   **WALSINGHAM, E.**; Aldborough, B.
Melusine Baroness of Schulenberg.
For life.
C 231/10, p. 20; 8 Geo. I, pt. 4 (C 66/3548) no. 20.

1722 23 May   **GRAHAM, E.**; Graham, B.
David Graham *styled* Marquess of Graham, eldest son
of James Duke of Montrose (S).
Remainder, failing heirs male, to Lord William
Graham and Lord George Graham, second and third
sons of said Duke of Montrose and their heirs male
respectively.
C 231/10, p. 23; 8 Geo. I, pt. 4 (C 66/3548) no. 18.

1722 24 May   **KER, E.**; Ker, B.
Robert Ker *styled* Marquess of Bowmont, eldest son
of John Duke of Roxburghe (S).
C 231/10, p. 22; 8 Geo. I, pt. 4 (C 66/3548) no. 19.

1723 1 June   **WALPOLE, B.**
Robert Walpole, eldest son of Robert Walpole, the
elder.
Remainder, failing heirs male, to Edward Walpole and
Horatio Walpole, second and third sons of elder Robert
Walpole and their heirs male respectively; failing whom
to their father Robert Walpole and his heirs male;
failing whom to heirs male of Robert Walpole, father of
elder Robert.
C 231/10, p. 44; 9 Geo. I, pt. 3 (C 66/3553) no. 13.

1725 29 May   **KING, B.**
Sir Peter King, Kt.
C 231/10, p. 80; 11 Geo. I, pt. 3 (C 66/3559) no. 29.

1726 26 July   **EDINBURGH, D.**; Ely, M.; Eltham, E.;
Launceston, V.; Snowdon, B.
Prince Frederick Lewis.
C 231/10, p. 101; 12 Geo. I, pt. 2 (C 66/3561) no. 5.

1726 27 July   **CUMBERLAND, D.**; Berkhamstead, M.;
Kennington, E.; Trematon, V.; Alderney, B.
Prince William.
C 231/10, p. 101; 12 Geo. I, pt. 2 (C 66/3561) no. 6.

George II

1728 8 Jan.   **WILMINGTON, B.**
Hon. Sir Spencer Compton, Kt.
C 231/10, p. 136; 1 Geo. II, pt. 6 (C 66/3571) no. 36.

1728 28 May
9 a.m.   **HOBART, B.**
Sir John Hobart, Bart.
C 231/10, p. 149; 1 Geo. II, pt. 7 (C 66/3572) no. 47.

1728 28 May
10 a.m.   **MONSON, B.**
Sir John Monson, Bart.
C 231/10, p. 149; 1 Geo. II, pt. 7 (C 66/3572) no. 46.

1728 28 May 11 a.m.	**MALTON, B.** Sir Thomas Wentworth, Kt. C 231/10, p. 149; 1 Geo. II, pt. 6 (C 66/3571) no. 4.
1728 28 May 12 noon	**LOVEL, B.** Sir Thomas Coke, Kt. C 231/10, p. 149; 1 Geo. II, pt. 6 (C 66/3571) no. 3.
1729 8 Jan.	**WALES, P.**; Chester, E. Prince Frederick Lewis. Remainder to heirs, kings of Great Britain. C 231/10, p. 154; 2 Geo. II, pt. 2 (C 66/3576) no. 1.
1729 13 Sept.	**WALDEGRAVE, E.**; Chewton, V. James Lord Waldegrave. C 231/10, p. 163; 3 Geo. II, pt. 2 (C 66/3579) no. 5.
1730 6 Jan.	**HARRINGTON, B.** Hon. William Stanhope. C 231/10, p. 165; 3 Geo. II, pt. 1 (C 66/3578) no. 7.
1730 14 May	**ASHBURNHAM, E.**; St. Asaph, V. John Lord Ashburnham. C 231/10, p. 172; 3 Geo. II, pt. 3 (C 66/3580) no. 1.
1730 14 May	**FITZWALTER, E.**; Harwich, V. Benjamin Lord Fitzwalter. C 231/10, p. 172; 3 Geo. II, pt. 3 (C 66/3580) no. 10.
1730 14 May	**WILMINGTON, E.**; Pevensey, V. Spencer Lord Wilmington. C 231/10, p. 172; 3 Geo. II, pt. 3 (C 66/3580) no. 3.
1731 15 Jan.	**RAYMOND, B.** Sir Robert Raymond, Kt. C 231/10, p. 179; 4 Geo. II, pt. 3 (C 66/3583) no. 20.
1731 8 Dec.	**EFFINGHAM, E.** Francis Lord Howard. C 231/10, p. 187; 5 Geo. II, pt. 1 (C 66/3584) no. 16.
1733 23 Nov.	**HARDWICKE, B.** Sir Philip Yorke, Kt. C 231/10, p. 208; 7 Geo. II, pt. 2 (C 66/3591) no. 16.

1733 5 Dec.

TALBOT, B.
Charles Talbot.
C 231/10, p. 209; 7 Geo. II, pt. 2 (C 66/3591)
no. 12.

1734 19 Nov.

MALTON, E.; Higham, V.; Wath, B.
Thomas Lord Malton.
C 231/10, p. 223; 8 Geo. II, pt. 2 (C 66/3594)
no. 16.

1735 23 Jan.

GODOLPHIN, B.
Francis Earl of Godolphin.
Remainder, failing heirs male, to heirs male of Henry
Godolphin, late dean of St. Paul's.
C 231/10, p. 224; 8 Geo. II, pt. 2 (C 66/3594) no. 7.

1740 24 Mar.

YARMOUTH, E.; Yarmouth, B.
Amalie Sophie de Wallmoden.
For life.
C 231/10, p. 298; 13 Geo. II, pt. 2 (C 66/3602) no.
29 where dated 22 (*sic*) Mar.

1740 19 May

GREY, M.
Henry Duke of Kent.
Remainder, failing heirs male, to granddaughter, Lady
Jemima Campbell and heirs male.
C 231/10, p. 302; 13 Geo. II, pt. 2 (C 66/3602) no. 11
where dated 17 (*sic*) May.

1741 9 May

MONTFORT, B.
Henry Bromley.
C 231/10, p. 318; 14 Geo. II, pt. 3 (C 66/3605)
no. 11.

1741 11 May

ILCHESTER, B.
Stephen Fox.
C 231/10, p. 318; 14 Geo. II, pt. 3 (C 66/3605)
no. 10 where dated 9 (*sic*) May.

1741 12 May

CHEDWORTH, B.
John Howe.
C 231/10, p. 318; 14 Geo. II, pt. 3 (C 66/3605)
no. 12 where dated 9 (*sic*) May.

1742 6 Feb.   **ORFORD, E.**; Walpole, V.; Houghton, B.
Sir Robert Walpole, Kt.
C 231/10, p. 330; 15 Geo. II, pt. 2 (C 66/3607) no. 7.

1742 9 Feb.   **HARRINGTON, E.**; Petersham, V.
William Lord Harrington.
C 231/10, p. 331; 15 Geo. II, pt. 2 (C 66/3607) no. 8.

1742 19 Apr.   **FITZWILLIAM, B.**
William Earl Fitzwilliam (I).
C 231/10, p. 338; 15 Geo. II, pt. 2 (C 66/3607) no. 4.

1742 20 Apr.   **EDGCUMBE, B.**
Richard Edgcumbe.
C 231/10, p. 338; 15 Geo. II, pt. 2 (C 66/3607) no. 5.

1742 14 July   **BATH, E.**; Pulteney, V.; Hedon, B.
William Pulteney.
C 231/10, p. 341; LP 16 Geo. II enrolled 15 (*sic*) Geo. II,
pt. 2 (C 66/3607) no. 6.

1743 11 Apr.   **PORTSMOUTH, E.**
John Viscount Lymington.
C 231/10, p. 352; 16 Geo. II (C 66/3612) no. 22.

1743 20 Dec.   **SANDYS, B.**
Samuel Sandys.
C 231/10, p. 360; 17 Geo. II, pt. 1 (C 66/3613)
no. 25.

1743 21 Dec.   **HERBERT, B.**
Henry Arthur Herbert.
C 231/10, p. 360; 17 Geo. II, pt. 1 (C 66/3613)
no. 24.

1744 9 May   **LEICESTER, E.**; Coke, V.
Thomas Lord Lovel.
C 231/10, p. 368; 17 Geo. II, pt. 1 (C 66/3613) no. 9.

1746 17 Apr.   **BRUCE, B.**
Charles Earl of Ailesbury.
Remainder, failing heirs male, to nephew, Hon.
Thomas Bruce Brudenell, brother of George Earl of
Cardigan and heirs male.
C 231/10, p. 402; 19 Geo. II, pt. 2 (C 66/3618)
no. 11.

1746 19 Apr.

ROCKINGHAM, M.
Thomas Earl of Rockingham.
C 231/10, p. 402; 19 Geo. II, pt. 2 (C 66/3618)
no. 10.

1746 5 July

CLINTON, E.; Fortescue, B.
Hugh Lord Clinton.
Remainder (for earldom) to heirs male; (for barony) to
same; failing whom to brother Matthew Fortescue and
heirs male.
C 231/10, p. 407; 20 Geo. II, pt. 1 (C 66/3619)
no. 24.

1746 7 July

BROOKE, E.
Francis Lord Brooke.
C 231/10, p. 407; 20 Geo. II, pt. 1 (C 66/3619)
no. 22.

1746 8 July

GOWER, E.; Trentham, V.
John Lord Gower.
C 231/10, p. 407; 20 Geo. II, pt. 1 (C 66/3619)
no. 21.

1746 5 Sept.

BUCKINGHAMSHIRE, E.
John Lord Hobart.
C 231/10, p. 410; 20 Geo. II, pt. 1 (C 66/3619) no. 4.

1746 6 Sept.

FITZWILLIAM, E.; Milton, V.
William Earl Fitzwilliam (I) & Lord Fitzwilliam (GB).
C 231/10, p. 411; 20 Geo. II, pt. 1 (C 66/3619) no. 3.

1747 12 Jan.

ILCHESTER, B.
Stephen Lord Ilchester.
Remainder, failing heirs male, to brother Henry Fox
and heirs male.
C 231/11, p. 5; 20 Geo. II, pt. 2 (C 66/3621) no. 8.

1747 21 Feb.

LEINSTER, V.
James Earl of Kildare (I).
C 231/11, p. 7; 20 Geo. II, pt. 2 (C 66/3621) no. 4.

1747 13 June

ANSON, B.
George Anson.
C 231/11, p. 12; 21 Geo. II, pt. 1 (C 66/3622) no. 30.

1747 29 June   **RAVENSWORTH, B.**
                      Sir Henry Liddell, Bart.
                      C 231/11, p. 15; 21 Geo. II, pt. 1 (C 66/3622) no. 13.

1747 29 June   **FOLKESTONE, V.**; Longford, B.
                      Sir Jacob Bouverie, Bart.
                      C 231/11, p. 16; 21 Geo. II, pt. 1 (C 66/3622) no. 15.

1747 7 July   **FEVERSHAM, B.**
                      Anthony Duncombe.
                      C 231/11, p. 16; 21 Geo. II, pt. 1 (C 66/3622) no. 11;
                      dated 23 June (*sic*) in *CP*, v, 366.

1747 14 July   **ARCHER, B.**
                      Thomas Archer.
                      C 231/11, p. 17; 21 Geo. II, pt. 1 (C 66/3622) no. 8.

1748 8 Jan.   **ROLLE, B.**
                      Henry Rolle.
                      C 231/11, p. 31; 21 Geo. II, pt. 3 (C 66/3624) no. 24.

1748 27 May   **POWIS, E.**; Ludlow, V.; Powis, B.
                      Henry Arthur Lord Herbert.
                      C 231/11, p. 45; 21 Geo. II, pt. 2 (C 66/3623) no. 6.

1749 12 June   **PONSONBY, B.**
                      Brabazon Earl of Bessborough (I).
                      C 231/11, p. 65; 23 Geo. II, pt. 1 (C 66/3627) no. 14.

1749 2 Oct.   **NORTHUMBERLAND, E.**; Warkworth, B.
                      Algernon Duke of Somerset.
                      Remainder, failing heirs male, to Sir Hugh Smithson,
                      Bart. and heirs male by his wife Lady Elizabeth Smithson,
                      daughter of said Duke of Somerset; failing whom to said
                      Lady Elizabeth Smithson and heirs male.
                      C 231/11, p. 69; 23 Geo. II, pt. 2 (C 66/3628) no. 22.

1749 3 Oct.   **EGREMONT, E.**; Cockermouth, B.
                      Algernon Duke of Somerset.
                      Remainder, failing heirs male, to nephew Sir Charles
                      Wyndham, Bart. and heirs male; failing whom to his
                      brother, Percy Wyndham O'Brien and heirs male.
                      C 231/11, p. 69; 23 Geo. II, pt. 2 (C 66/3628) no. 20.

1749 16 Oct.

HERBERT, B.
Henry Arthur Earl of Powis.
Remainder, failing heirs male, to brother Richard
Herbert and heirs male; failing whom to Francis Herbert
of Ludlow and heirs male.
C 231/11, p. 70; 23 Geo. II, pt. 2 (C 66/3628) no. 17.

1749 18 Oct.

TEMPLE, E.
Hester Viscountess Cobham.
C 231/11, p. 70; 23 Geo. II, pt. 2 (C 66/3628) no. 16.

1749 1 Dec.

HARCOURT, E.; Newnham, V.
Simon Viscount Harcourt.
C 231/11, p. 73; 23 Geo. II, pt. 2 (C 66/3628) no. 6.

1750 28 Mar.

VERE, B.
Lord Vere Beauclerk.
C 231/11, p. 83; 23 Geo. II, pt. 4 (C 66/3630) no. 11.

1750 3 Aug.

HERTFORD, E.; Beauchamp, V.
Francis Lord Conway.
Remainder, failing heirs male, to brother Hon. Henry
Conway and heirs male.
C 231/11, p. 89; 24 Geo. II, pt. 1 (C 66/3631) no. 10.

1751 20 Apr.

WALES, P.; Chester, E.
Prince George William Frederick Duke of Edinburgh.
Remainder to heirs, kings of Great Britain.
C 231/11, p. 98; 24 Geo. II, pt. 2 (C 66/3632) no. 15.

1752 8 Apr.

GUILFORD, E.
Francis Lord North & Guilford.
C 231/11, p. 117; 25 Geo. II, pt. 4 (C 66/3636)
no. 11.

1753 30 June

CORNWALLIS, E.; Brome, V.
Charles Lord Cornwallis.
C 231/11, p. 131; 27 Geo. II, pt. 1 (C 66/3640)
no. 12.

1754 2 Apr.

HARDWICKE, E.; Royston, V.
Philip Lord Hardwicke.
C 231/11, p. 141; 27 Geo. II, pt. 3 (C 66/3642)
no. 11.

1754 3 Apr.   **DARLINGTON, E.**; Barnard, V.
                            Henry Lord Barnard.
                            C 231/11, p. 141; 27 Geo. II, pt. 3 (C 66/3642)
                            no. 10.

1756 3 June   **HYDE, B.**
                            Hon. Thomas Villiers.
                            Remainder to heirs male by present wife, Lady
                            Charlotte Hyde; failing whom to said Lady Charlotte
                            Hyde and heirs male.
                            C 231/11, p. 185; 29 Geo. II, pt. 4 (C 66/3652)
                            no. 7.

1756 4 June   **WALPOLE, B.**
                            Horatio Walpole.
                            C 231/11, p. 186; 29 Geo. II, pt. 4 (C 66/3652) no. 6.

1756 16 June   **FAUCONBERG, E.**
                            Thomas Viscount Fauconberg.
                            C 231/11, p. 186; 29 Geo. II, pt. 4 (C 66/3652) no. 4.

1756 17 June   **ILCHESTER, E.**
                            Stephen Lord Ilchester.
                            Remainder, failing heirs male, to brother, Henry Fox,
                            and heirs male.
                            C 231/11, p. 186; 29 Geo. II, pt. 4 (C 66/3652) no. 3.

1756 8 Nov.   **MANSFIELD, B.**
                            Hon. William Murray.
                            C 231/11, p. 192; 30 Geo. II, pt. 2 (C 66/3654)
                            no. 21.

1756 17 Nov.   **NEWCASTLE UNDER LINE, D.**
                            Thomas Holles Duke of Newcastle upon Tyne.
                            Remainder, failing heirs male, to Henry Earl of
                            Lincoln and heirs male by Catherine Pelham, his present
                            wife.
                            C 231/11, p. 193; 30 Geo. II, pt. 2 (C 66/3654)
                            no. 11.

1756 17 Nov.   **HARWICH, B.**
                            Wills Earl of Hillsborough (I).
                            C 231/11, p. 193; 30 Geo. II, pt. 2 (C 66/3654)
                            no. 10.

1756 18 Nov.   **LYTTELTON, B.**
Sir George Lyttelton, Bart.
C 231/11, p. 193; 30 Geo., II, pt. 2 (C 66/3654)
no. 6.

1759 30 Nov.   **WARWICK, E.**
Francis Earl Brooke.
C 231/11, p. 252; 33 Geo. II, pt. 2 (C 66/3666)
no. 10; dated 13 (*sic*) Nov. in *CP*, ii, 335 and *ibid.*, xii,
pt. 2, 419.

1760 27 Mar.   **HENLEY, B.**
Sir Robert Henley, Kt.
C 231/11, p. 258; 33 Geo. II, pt. 3 (C 66/3667) no. 1.

1760 1 Apr.   **YORK & ALBANY, D.**; Ulster, E. (I)
Prince Edward Augustus.
C 231/11, p. 258; 33 Geo. II, pt. 4 (C 66/3668)
no. 20.

1760 20 May   **WYCOMBE, B.**
John Petty Earl of Shelburne (I).
C 231/11, p. 262; 33 Geo. II, pt. 4 (C 66/3668)
no. 13.

1760 21 May   **STAWELL, B.**
Hon. Mary Legge.
Remainder to heirs male by present husband Hon.
Henry Bilson Legge.
C 231/11, p. 262; 33 Geo. II, pt. 4 (C 66/3668)
no. 12.

1760 22 May   **SONDES, B.**
Hon. Lewis Watson.
C 231/11, p. 262; 33 Geo. II, pt. 4 (C 66/3668)
no. 11.

George III

1761 18 Mar.   **DELAWARR, E.**; Cantelupe, V.
John Lord Delawarr.
C 231/11, p. 285; 1 Geo. III, pt. 5 (C 66/3674) no. 23
where dated 16 (*sic*) Mar.

1761 19 Mar.   **TALBOT, E.**
William Lord Talbot.
C 231/11, p. 286; 1 Geo. III, pt. 5 (C 66/3674) no. 12.

1761 3 Apr.   **SPENCER, V.**; Spencer, B.
John Spencer.
C 231/11, p. 289; 1 Geo. III, pt. 6 (C 66/3675)
no. 10.

1761 3 Apr.   **MOUNTSTUART, B.**
Mary Countess of Bute.
Remainder to heirs male by John Earl of Bute.
C 231/11, p. 289; 1 Geo. III, pt. 6 (C 66/3675) no. 9.

1761 6 Apr.   **MELCOMBE, B.**
George Dodington.
C 231/11, p. 290; 1 Geo. III, pt. 10 (C 66/3679)
no. 19.

1761 7 Apr.   **GRANTHAM, B.**
Sir Thomas Robinson, Kt.
C 231/11, p. 290; 1 Geo. III, pt. 10 (C 66/3679)
no. 18.

1761 8 Apr.   **GROSVENOR, B.**
Sir Richard Grosvenor, Bart.
C 231/11, p. 290; 1 Geo. III, pt. 10 (C 66/3679)
no. 17.

1761 9 Apr.   **SCARSDALE, B.**
Sir Nathaniel Curzon, Bart.
C 231/11, p. 291; 1 Geo. III, pt. 10 (C 66/3679)
no. 13.

1761 10 Apr.   **BOSTON, B.**
Sir William Irby, Bart.
C 231/11, p. 291; 1 Geo. III, pt. 10 (C 66/3679)
no. 12.

1761 4 Dec.   **CHATHAM, B.**
Lady Hester Pitt.
Remainder to heirs male by husband William Pitt.
C 231/11, p. 311; 2 Geo. III, pt. 1 (C 66/3682)
no. 24.

1762 5 May   **WENTWORTH, V.**
Edward Lord Wentworth.
C 231/11, p. 323; 2 Geo. III, pt. 2 (C 66/3683) no. 11.

1762 5 May   **PELHAM, B.**
Thomas Holles Duke of Newcastle upon Tyne.
Remainder, failing heirs male, to Thomas Pelham of Stanmer, Sussex, and heirs male.
C 231/11, p. 323; 2 Geo. III, pt. 2 (C 66/3683) no. 10; dated 4 (*sic*) May in *CP*, ix, 531 and *ibid.*, x, 347.

1762 6 May   **COURTENAY, V.**
Sir William Courtenay, Bart.
C 231/11, p. 324; 2 Geo. III, pt. 2 (C 66/3683) no. 9.

1762 6 May   **HOLLAND, B.**
Lady Caroline Fox.
Remainder to heirs male by husband Henry Fox.
C 231/11, p. 324; 2 Geo. III, pt. 2 (C 66/3683) no. 8; dated 3 (*sic*) May in *CP*, vi, 541.

1762 7 May   **LOVEL & HOLLAND, B.**
John Earl of Egmont (I).
C 231/11, p. 324; 2 Geo. III, pt. 2 (C 66/3683) no. 7.

1762 8 May   **MONTAGU, B.**
John Montagu *styled* Lord Brudenell eldest son of George Earl of Cardigan.
C 231/11, p. 324; 2 Geo. III, pt. 3 (C 66/3684) no. 33.

1762 10 May   **MILTON, B.**
Joseph Lord Milton (I).
C 231/11, p. 324; 2 Geo. III, pt. 3 (C 66/3684) no. 32; dated 10 or 11 (*sic*) May in *CP*, vi, 541.

1762 11 May   **BEAULIEU, B.**
Sir Edward Montagu, Kt.
Remainder to heirs male by present wife, Isabella Duchess Dowager of Manchester.
C 231/11, p. 324; 2 Geo. III, pt. 3 (C 66/3684) no. 31.

1762 12 May   **VERNON, B.**
George Venables Vernon.
C 231/11, p. 325; 2 Geo. III, pt. 3 (C 66/3684) no. 30.

1762 13 May   **BINGLEY, B.**
                             George Lane.
                             Remainder to heirs male by present wife Harriot
                             daughter of Robert Lord Bingley deceased.
                             C 231/11, p. 325; 2 Geo. III, pt. 3 (C 66/3684) no. 29.

1762 19 Aug.   **WALES, P.**; Chester, E.
                             Prince George Augustus Frederick.
                             Remainder to heirs, kings of Great Britain.
                             C 231/11, p. 330; 2 Geo. III, pt. 4 (C 66/3685) no. 9.

1763 16 Apr.   **HOLLAND, B.**
                             Henry Fox.
                             C 231/11, p. 344; 3 Geo. III, pt. 2 (C 66/3687) no. 9;
                             dated 17 (*sic*) Apr. in *CP*, vi, 541.

1763 21 Apr.   **DUDLEY & WARD, V.**
                             John Lord Ward.
                             C 231/11, p. 347; 3 Geo. III, pt. 2 (C 66/3687) no. 5.

1763 27 Apr.   **DUCIE, B.**
                             Matthew Lord Ducie.
                             Remainder, failing heirs male, to nephews Thomas
                             Reynolds and Francis Reynolds and their heirs male
                             respectively.
                             C 231/11, p. 347; 3 Geo. III, pt. 5 (C 66/3690)
                             no. 12.

1763 27 Apr.   **LIGONIER, B.**
                             John Viscount Ligonier (I).
                             C 231/11, p. 348; 3 Geo. III, pt. 2 (C 66/3687) no. 2.

1764 19 May   **NORTHINGTON, E.**
                             Robert Lord Henley.
                             C 231/12, p. 16; 4 Geo. III, pt. 4 (C 66/3696) no. 16.

1764 19 Nov.   **GLOUCESTER & EDINBURGH, D.**;
                             Connaught, E. (I)
                             Prince William Henry.
                             C 231/12, p. 21; 5 Geo. III, pt. 1 (C 66/3698) no. 21.

1765 17 July   **CAMDEN, B.**
                             Sir Charles Pratt, Kt.
                             C 231/12, p. 33; 5 Geo. III, pt. 4 (C 66/3701) no. 7.

1765 19 Aug.

DIGBY, B.
Henry Lord Digby (I).
Remainder, failing heirs male, to heirs male of father, Edward Digby.
C 231/12, p. 34; 5 Geo. III, pt. 5 (C 66/3702) no. 3; dated 13 or 19 (*sic*) Aug. in *CP*, iv, 355.

1765 31 Oct.

RADNOR, E.; Pleydell Bouverie, B.
William Viscount Folkestone.
Remainder (for earldom) failing heirs male to heirs male of Jacob Viscount Folkestone; (for barony) to heirs male.
C 231/12, p. 36; 6 Geo. III, pt. 1 (C 66/3704) no. 21.

1765 1 Nov.

SPENCER, E.; Althorp, V.
John Viscount Spencer.
C 231/12, p. 36; 6 Geo. III, pt. 1 (C 66/3704) no. 20.

1766 4 Aug.

CHATHAM, E.; Pitt, V.
William Pitt.
C 231/12, p. 54; 6 Geo. III, pt. 4 (C 66/3707) no. 6.

1766 10 Sept.

LIGONIER, E.
John Viscount Ligonier (I) & Lord Ligonier (GB).
C 231/12, p. 56; 6 Geo. III, pt. 5 (C 66/3708) no. 2.

1766 22 Oct.

CUMBERLAND & STRATHEARN, D.; Dublin, E. (I)
Prince Henry Frederick.
C 231/12, p. 57; 6 Geo. III, pt. 6 (C 66/3709) no. 3.

1766 22 Oct.

NORTHUMBERLAND, D.; Percy, E.
Hugh Earl of Northumberland.
Remainder to heirs male by Elizabeth, his present wife.
C 231/12, p. 57; 6 Geo. III, pt. 6 (C 66/3709) no. 2.

1766 28 Oct.

MAYNARD, V.; Maynard, B.
Charles Lord Maynard.
Remainder, failing heirs male, to Sir William Maynard, Bart. and heirs male.
C 231/12, p. 57; 7 Geo. III, pt. 1 (C 66/3710) no. 18.

1766 5 Nov.

MONTAGU, D.; Monthermer, M.
George Earl of Cardigan.
C 231/12, p. 58; 7 Geo. III, pt. 1 (C 66/3710) no. 17.

1766 22 Dec.

SUNDRIDGE, B.

John Campbell *styled* Marquess of Lorne, eldest son of John Duke of Argyll (S).

Remainder, failing heirs male, to brothers Lord Frederick Campbell and Lord William Campbell and their heirs male respectively.

C 231/12, p. 63; 7 Geo. III, pt. 2 (C 66/3711) no. 12.

1767 19 Aug.

GREENWICH, B.

Caroline Countess of Dalkeith.

Remainder to heirs male by husband, Hon. Charles Townshend.

C 231/12, p. 70; 7 Geo. III, pt. 5 (C 66/3714) no. 16.

1770 19 Jan.

MORDEN, B.

Hon. Charles Yorke.

C 231/12, p. 103; LP not sealed.

1771 24 Jan.

APSLEY, B.

Hon. Henry Bathurst.

C 231/12, p. 118; 11 Geo. III, pt. 3 (C 66/3730) no. 27.

1772 27 Aug.

BATHURST, E.

Allen Lord Bathurst.

C 231/12, p. 146; 12 Geo. III, pt. 4 (C 66/3737) no. 6.

1772 28 Aug.

HILLSBOROUGH, E.; Fairford, V.

Wills Earl of Hillsborough (I) and Lord Harwich (GB).

C 231/12, p. 146; 12 Geo. III, pt. 4 (C 66/3737) no. 3.

1776 20 May

HAMILTON, B.

Elizabeth Duchess of Argyll.

C 231/12, p. 205; 16 Geo. III, pt. 4 (C 66/3759) no. 12.

1776 20 May

HUME, B.

Alexander Hume Campbell *styled* Lord Polwarth, eldest son of Hugh Earl of Marchmont (S).

C 231/12, p. 205; 16 Geo. III, pt. 4 (C 66/3759) no. 3.

1776 20 May

CARDIFF, B.

John Stuart *styled* Lord Mountstuart, eldest son of John Earl of Bute (S).

C 231/12, p. 206; 16 Geo. III, pt. 4 (C 66/3759) no. 4.

1776 20 May	**HAWKE, B.** Sir Edward Hawke, Kt. C 231/12, p. 206; 16 Geo. III, pt. 4 (C 66/3759) no. 5.
1776 20 May	**CRANLEY, B.** George Onslow. C 231/12, p. 206; 16 Geo. III, pt. 4 (C 66/3759) no. 7.
1776 20 May	**AMHERST, B.** Sir Jeffrey Amherst, Kt. C 231/12, p. 206; 16 Geo. III, pt. 4 (C 66/3759) no. 6.
1776 20 May	**BROWNLOW, B.** Sir Brownlow Cust, Bart. C 231/12, p. 206; 16 Geo. III, pt. 4 (C 66/3759) no. 8.
1776 20 May	**RIVERS, B.** George Pitt. C 231/12, p. 206; 16 Geo. III, pt. 4 (C 66/3759) no. 9.
1776 20 May	**HARROWBY, B.** Nathaniel Ryder. C 231/12, p. 207; 16 Geo. III, pt. 4 (C 66/3759) no. 10.
1776 20 May	**FOLEY, B.** Thomas Foley. C 231/12, p. 207; 16 Geo. III, pt. 4 (C 66/3759) no. 11.
1776 10 June	**AILESBURY, E.** Thomas Lord Bruce. C 231/12, p. 207; 16 Geo. III, pt. 5 (C 66/3760) no. 12.
1776 14 June	**CLARENDON, E.** Thomas Lord Hyde. Remainder to heirs male by Charlotte present wife. C 231/12, p. 208; 16 Geo. III, pt. 5 (C 66/3760) no. 11.
1776 14 June	**HAMPDEN, V.** Robert Lord Trevor. C 231/12, p. 208; 16 Geo. III, pt. 5 (C 66/3760) no. 10.

1776 31 Oct.

MANSFIELD, E.
William Lord Mansfield.
Remainder, failing heirs male, to Louisa Viscountess Stormont and heirs male by husband David Viscount Stormont (S).
C 231/12, p. 213; 17 Geo. III, pt. 1 (C 66/3762) no. 14.

1778 3 June

THURLOW, B.
Edward Thurlow.
C 231/12, p. 238; 18 Geo. III, pt. 3 (C 66/3769) no. 4.

1780 14 June

LOUGHBOROUGH, B.
Alexander Wedderburn.
C 231/12, p. 269; 20 Geo. III, pt. 4 (C 66/3780) no. 21.

1780 17 Oct.

DINEVOR, B.
William Earl Talbot.
For life with remainder to daughter Lady Cecil Rice and heirs male.
C 231/12, p. 278; LP 20 Geo. III enrolled 21 (*sic*) Geo. III, pt. 1 (C 66/3782) no. 18.

1780 17 Oct.

GAGE, B.
William Hall Viscount Gage (I).
C 231/12, p. 278; LP 20 Geo. III enrolled 21 (*sic*) Geo. III, pt. 1 (C 66/3782) no. 17.

1780 17 Oct.

BRUDENELL, B.
Hon. James Brudenell.
C 231/12, p. 278; LP 20 Geo. III enrolled 21 (*sic*) Geo. III, pt. 1 (C 66/3782) no. 13.

1780 17 Oct.

WALSINGHAM, B.
Sir William de Grey, Kt.
C 231/12, p. 278; LP 20 Geo. III enrolled 21 (*sic*) Geo. III, pt. 1 (C 66/3782) no. 15.

1780 17 Oct.

BAGOT, B.
Sir William Bagot, Bart.
C 231/12, p. 278; LP 20 Geo. III enrolled 21 (*sic*) Geo. III, pt. 1 (C 66/3782) no. 14.

1780 17 Oct. **SOUTHAMPTON, B.**
Charles Fitzroy.
C 231/12, p. 279; LP 20 Geo. III enrolled 21 (*sic*)
Geo. III, pt. 1 (C 66/3782) no. 16.

1780 17 Oct. **PORCHESTER, B.**
Henry Herbert.
C 231/12, p. 279; LP 20 Geo. III enrolled 21 (*sic*)
Geo. III, pt. 1 (C 66/3782) no. 12.

1781 5 Mar. **MOUNT EDGCUMBE & VALLETORT, V.**
George Lord Edgcumbe.
C 231/12, p. 286; 21 Geo. III, pt. 4 (C 66/3785)
no. 12.

1782 11 Feb. **SACKVILLE, V.**; Bolebrooke, B.
Lord George Germain.
C 231/12, p. 300; 22 Geo. III, pt. 3 (C 66/3791)
no. 15.

1782 8 Apr. **ASHBURTON, B.**
John Dunning.
C 231/12, p. 306; 22 Geo. III, pt. 5 (C 66/3793)
no. 14.

1782 9 Apr. **GRANTLEY, B.**
Sir Fletcher Norton, Kt.
C 231/12, p. 307; 22 Geo. III, pt. 5 (C 66/3793)
no. 13.

1782 20 Apr. **HOWE, V.**
Richard Viscount Howe (I).
C 231/12, p. 311; 22 Geo. III, pt. 6 (C 66/3794)
no. 10.

1782 22 Apr. **KEPPEL, V.**
Hon. Augustus Keppel.
C 231/12, p. 311; 22 Geo. III, pt. 6 (C 66/3794)
no. 9.

1782 19 June **RODNEY, B.**
Sir George Bridges Rodney, Kt.
C 231/12, p. 315; 22 Geo. III, pt. 8 (C 66/3796)
no. 13.

1783 5 Mar.

RAWDON, B.
Francis Rawdon *styled* Lord Rawdon, eldest son of John Earl of Moira (I).
C 231/12, p. 329; 23 Geo. III, pt. 4 (C 66/3802) no. 10.

1783 6 Mar.

SYDNEY, B.
Thomas Townshend.
C 231/12, p. 329; 23 Geo. III, pt. 4 (C 66/3802) no. 9.

1784 5 Jan.

CAMELFORD, B.
Thomas Pitt.
C 231/12, p. 348; 24 Geo. III, pt. 3 (C 66/3809) no. 14.

1784 28 Jan.

LOVAINE, B.
Hugh Duke of Northumberland.
For life with remainder to Lord Algernon Percy and heirs male.
C 231/12, p. 350; 24 Geo. III, pt. 4 (C 66/3810) no. 6.

1784 29 Jan.

CARTERET, B.
Hon. Henry Frederick Carteret.
Remainder, failing heirs male, to Hon. George Thynne, second son of Thomas Viscount Weymouth and heirs male; failing whom to Hon. John Thynne, third son of the said Viscount and heirs male; failing whom to the fourth, fifth, sixth, seventh and any other son of said Viscount and their heirs male respectively.
C 231/12, p. 350; 24 Geo. III, pt. 4 (C 66/3810) no. 3.

1784 30 Jan.

ELIOT, B.
Edward Eliot.
C 231/12, p. 351; 24 Geo. III, pt. 4 (C 66/3810) no. 1.

1784 14 May

BULKELEY, B.
Thomas Viscount Bulkeley (I).
C 231/12, p. 361; 24 Geo. III, pt. 6 (C 66/3812) no. 8.

1784 15 May

GREY DE WILTON, B.
Sir Thomas Egerton, Bart.
C 231/12, p. 361; 24 Geo. III, pt. 6 (C 66/3812) no. 7.

1784 17 May   **SOMERS, B.**
Sir Charles Cocks, Bart.
C 231/12, p. 361; 24 Geo. III, pt. 6 (C 66/3812)
no. 6.

1784 17 May   **ABERGAVENNY, E.**; Nevill, V.
George Lord Abergavenny.
C 231/12, p. 362; 24 Geo. III, pt. 6 (C 66/3812)
no. 5.

1784 18 May   **LEICESTER, E.**
George Lord Ferrers.
C 231/12, p. 362; 24 Geo. III, pt. 7 (C 66/3813)
no. 20.

1784 18 May   **BORINGDON, B.**
John Parker.
C 231/12, p. 362; 24 Geo. III, pt. 7 (C 66/3813)
no. 21.

1784 19 May   **BERWICK, B.**
Noel Hill.
C 231/12, p. 362; 24 Geo. III, pt. 7 (C 66/3813)
no. 16.

1784 19 May   **UXBRIDGE, E.**
Henry Lord Paget.
C 231/12, p. 362; 24 Geo. III, pt. 7 (C 66/3813)
no. 17.

1784 20 May   **SHERBORNE, B.**
James Dutton.
C 231/12, p. 362; 24 Geo. III, pt. 7 (C 66/3813)
no. 14.

1784 24 May   **LONSDALE, E.**; Lowther, V.; Lonsdale, V.; Lowther, B.
Sir James Lowther, Bart.
C 231/12, p. 363; 24 Geo. III, pt. 7 (C 66/3813)
no. 11.

1784 2 July   **NORWICH, E.**; Gordon, B.
Alexander Duke of Gordon (S).
C 231/12, p. 366; 24 Geo. III, pt. 7 (C 66/3813) no. 4;
dated 7 (*sic*) July in *CP*, vi, 5 and *ibid.*, ix, 778.

1784 3 July   **TALBOT, E.**; Ingestre, V.
John Lord Talbot.
C 231/12, p. 366; 24 Geo. III, pt. 7 (C 66/3813)
no. 3.

1784 5 July   **GROSVENOR, E.**; Belgrave, V.
Richard Lord Grosvenor.
C 231/12, p. 366; 24 Geo. III, pt. 8 (C 66/3814)
no. 17.

1784 8 July   **BEAULIEU, E.**
Edward Lord Beaulieu.
C 231/12, p. 367; 24 Geo. III, pt. 8 (C 66/3814)
no. 15.

1784 29 Nov.   **YORK & ALBANY, D.**; Ulster, E. (I)
Prince Frederick.
C 231/12, p. 371; 25 Geo. III, pt. 1 (C 66/3816) no. 3;
dated 27 (*sic*) Nov. in *CP*, xii, pt. 2, 921.

1784 4 Dec.   **BUCKINGHAM, M.**
George Earl Temple.
C 231/12, p. 372; 25 Geo. III, pt. 1 (C 66/3816)
no. 2.

1784 6 Dec.   **LANSDOWNE, M.**; Wycombe, E.; Calne, V.
William Earl of Shelburne (I) and Lord Wycombe
(GB).
C 231/12, p. 372; 25 Geo. III, pt. 2 (C 66/3817)
no. 14.

1786 1 Mar.   **STAFFORD, M.**
Granville Earl Gower.
C 231/12, p. 389; warrant dated 28 Feb. enrolled 26
Geo. III, pt. 4 (C 66/3825) no. 13.

1786 13 May   **CAMDEN, E.**; Bayham, V.
Charles Lord Camden.
C 231/12, p. 397; 26 Geo. III, pt. 5 (C 66/3826) no. 1.

1786 18 Aug.   **STRANGE, E.**; Murray, B.
John Duke of Atholl (S).
C 231/12, p. 402; warrant dated 15 Aug. enrolled 26
Geo. III, pt. 9 (C 66/3830) no. 19.

1786 21 Aug. **DOUGLAS, B.**
William Duke of Queensberry (S).
C 231/12, p. 402; warrant dated 15 Aug. enrolled 26
Geo. III, pt. 9 (C 66/3830) no. 10.

1786 21 Aug. **MONTAGU, B.**
George Duke of Montagu.
For life with remainder to Lord Henry James Scott,
second son of Henry Duke of Buccleuch by his wife
Elizabeth daughter of said George Duke of Montagu and
heirs male; failing whom to third, fourth, fifth and any
other sons of Elizabeth Duchess of Buccleuch and heirs
male respectively.
C 231/12, p. 402; warrant dated 15 Aug. enrolled 26
Geo. III, pt. 9 (C 66/3830) no. 18.

1786 21 Aug. **TYRONE, B.**
George de la Poer Earl of Tyrone (I).
C 231/12, p. 402; warrant dated 15 Aug. enrolled 26
Geo. III, pt. 9 (C 66/3830) no. 11.

1786 21 Aug. **CARLETON, B.**
Richard Earl of Shannon (I).
C 231/12, p. 402; warrant dated 15 Aug. enrolled 26
Geo. III, pt. 9 (C 66/3830) no. 15; dated 6 (*sic*) Aug. in
CP, iii, 27 and *ibid.*, xi, 658.

1786 21 Aug. **DELAVAL, B.**
John Hussey Lord Delaval (I).
C 231/12, p. 402; warrant dated 15 Aug. enrolled 26
Geo. III, pt. 9 (C 66/3830) no. 12.

1786 21 Aug. **HAWKESBURY, B.**
Charles Jenkinson.
C 231/12, p. 403; warrant dated 15 Aug. enrolled 26
Geo. III, pt. 9 (C 66/3830) no. 13.

1786 21 Aug. **SUFFIELD, B.**
Sir Harbord Harbord, Bart.
C 231/12, p. 403; warrant dated 15 Aug. enrolled 26
Geo. III, pt. 9 (C 66/3830) no. 16.

1786 21 Aug. **DORCHESTER, B.**
Sir Guy Carleton, Kt.
C 231/12, p. 403; warrant dated 15 Aug. enrolled 26
Geo. III, pt. 9 (C 66/3830) no. 14.

1786 24 Aug.   **HAMILTON, V.**
                        James Earl of Abercorn (S).
                        Remainder, failing heirs male, to James Hamilton son
                        of John Hamilton, late brother of James Earl of Abercorn.
                        C 231/12, p. 403; warrant dated 15 Aug. enrolled 26
                        Geo. III, pt. 9 (C 66/3830) no. 17.

1787 6 July   **HEATHFIELD, B.**
                        Sir George Augustus Eliott, Kt.
                        C 231/12, p. 420; 27 Geo. III, pt. 7 (C 66/3837)
                        no. 7.

1787 31 Oct.   **TOWNSHEND, M.**
                        George Viscount Townshend.
                        C 231/13, p. 1; 28 Geo. III, pt. 7 (C 66/3845) no. 2
                        where dated 29 (*sic*) Oct.

1788 9 June   **KENYON, B.**
                        Sir Lloyd Kenyon, Bart.
                        C 231/13, p. 14; 28 Geo. III, pt. 5 (C 66/3843)
                        no. 3.

1788 19 Aug.   **HOWE, E.**; Howe, B.
                        Richard Viscount Howe (I & GB).
                        Remainder, failing heirs male, to daughters, Sophia
                        Charlotte Curzon, Mary Juliana Howe and Catherine
                        Louisa Countess of Altamont and their heirs male
                        respectively.
                        C 231/13, p. 19; 28 Geo. III, pt. 6 (C 66/3844) no. 3
                        where dated 16 (*sic*) Aug.

1788 5 Sept.   **BRAYBROOKE, B.**
                        John Griffin Lord Howard of Walden.
                        Remainder, failing heirs male, to Richard Aldworth
                        Neville of Billingbear, Berks and heirs male.
                        C 231/13, p. 19; 28 Geo. III, pt. 1 (C 66/3839) no. 9
                        where dated 3 (*sic*) Sept.

1788 6 Sept.   **AMHERST, B.**
                        Jeffrey Lord Amherst.
                        Remainder, failing heirs male, to nephew William Pitt
                        Amherst and heirs male.
                        C 231/13, p. 19; 28 Geo. III, pt. 1 (C 66/3839) no. 7
                        where dated 3 (*sic*) Sept.

1788 18 Sept.

DOVER, B.
Sir Joseph Yorke, Kt.
C 231/13, p. 20; 28 Geo. III, pt. 1 (C 66/3839) no. 4
where dated 16 (*sic*) Sept.

1788 19 Sept.

MALMESBURY, B.
Sir James Harris, Kt.
C 231/13, p. 20; 28 Geo. III, pt. 1 (C 66/3839) no. 5
where dated 17 (*sic*) Sept.

1789 20 May

CLARENCE & ST. ANDREWS, D.; Munster, E. (I)
Prince William Henry.
C 231/13, p. 30; 29 Geo. III, pt. 2 (C 66/3847) no. 1.

1789 11 June

SYDNEY, V.
Thomas Lord Sydney.
C 231/13, p. 31; 29 Geo. III, pt. 3 (C 66/3848) no. 5.

1789 24 Aug.

SALISBURY, M.
James Earl of Salisbury.
C 231/13, p. 36; 29 Geo. III, pt. 5 (C 66/3850) no. 6
where dated 20 (*sic*) Aug.; dated 25 (*sic*) Aug. in *CP*, xi,
410.

1789 25 Aug.

BATH, M.
Thomas Viscount Weymouth.
C 231/13, p. 36; 29 Geo. III, pt. 5 (C 66/3850) no. 4
where dated 20 (*sic*) Aug.; dated 18 (*sic*) Aug. in *CP*, ii,
25.

1789 31 Aug.

MOUNT EDGCUMBE, E.
George Viscount Edgcumbe & Valletort.
C 231/13, p. 37; 29 Geo. III, pt. 6 (C 66/3851) no. 2
where dated 27 (*sic*) Aug.

1789 1 Sept.

FORTESCUE, E.; Ebrington, V.
Hugh Lord Fortescue.
C 231/13, p. 37; 29 Geo. III, pt. 6 (C 66/3851) no. 6
where dated 27 Aug. (*sic*).

1790 3 July

FISHERWICK, B.
Arthur Earl of Donegall (I).
C 231/13, p. 54; 30 Geo. III, pt. 7 (C 66/3860)
no. 11.

1790 5 July   **FIFE, B.**
James Earl Fife (I).
C 231/13, p. 54; 30 Geo. III, pt. 7 (C 66/3860) no. 10
where dated 3 (*sic*) July.

1790 6 July   **VERULAM, B.**
James Bucknall Viscount Grimston (I).
C 231/13, p. 54; 30 Geo. III, pt. 7 (C 66/3860) no. 7
where dated 3 (*sic*) July.

1790 7 July   **MULGRAVE, B.**
Constantine John Lord Mulgrave (I).
C 231/13, p. 54; 30 Geo. III, pt. 7 (C 66/3860) no. 6
where dated 3 (*sic*) July.

1790 8 July   **DOUGLAS, B.**
Archibald Douglas.
C 231/13, p. 55; 30 Geo. III, pt. 7 (C 66/3860) no. 5
where dated 3 (*sic*) July.

1790 9 July   **HAREWOOD, B.**
Edwin Lascelles.
C 231/13, p. 55; 30 Geo. III, pt. 8 (C 66/3861) no. 10
where dated 3 (*sic*) July.

1790 15 Oct.   **ABERCORN, M.**
John James Earl of Abercorn (S) & Viscount Hamilton
(GB).
C 231/13, p. 57; LP 30 Geo. III enrolled 31 (*sic*) Geo.
III, pt. 1 (C 66/3863) no. 13 where dated 12 (*sic*) Oct.

1790 1 Nov.   **GAGE, B.**
William Hall Viscount Gage (I) & Lord Gage (GB).
For life with remainder to nephew Henry Gage and
heirs male.
C 231/13, p. 57; 31 Geo. III, pt. 1 (C 66/3863) no. 1
where dated 30 Oct. (*sic*).

1790 1 Nov.   **DIGBY, E.**; Coleshill, V.
Henry Lord Digby (I & GB).
C 231/13, p. 57; 31 Geo. III, pt. 1 (C 66/3863) no. 2
where dated 30 Oct. (*sic*).

1790 2 Nov.   **BEVERLEY, E.**
Algernon Lord Lovaine.
C 231/13, p. 58; 31 Geo. III, pt. 1 (C 66/3863) no. 3
where dated 30 Oct. (*sic*).

1790 25 Nov.

GRENVILLE, B.
William Wyndham Grenville.
C 231/13, p. 59; 31 Geo. III, pt. 2 (C 66/3864) no. 8.

1791 11 Aug.

DOUGLAS, B.
George Earl of Morton (S).
C 231/13, p. 76; 31 Geo. III, pt. 9 (C 66/3871) no. 4
where dated 6 (*sic*) Aug.

1792 18 May

DORCHESTER, E.; Milton, V.
Joseph Lord Milton (I & GB).
C 231/13, p. 86; 32 Geo. III, pt. 8 (C 66/3880) no. 9.

1792 11 June

THURLOW, B.
Edward Lord Thurlow.
Remainder, failing heirs male, to (1) Edward Thurlow
and (2) Thomas Thurlow, sons of Thomas late Bishop of
Durham and (3) Edward South Thurlow, Prebendary of
Norwich and their heirs male respectively.
C 231/13, p. 87; 32 Geo. III, pt. 1 (C 66/3873)
no. 12.

1792 26 July

BATH, B.
Henrietta Laura Pulteney.
C 231/13, p. 90; 32 Geo. III, pt. 1 (C 66/3873) no. 2.

1792 1 Aug.

MANSFIELD, E.
William Earl of Mansfield.
Remainder, failing heirs male, to David Viscount
Stormont (S) and heirs male.
C 231/13, p. 90; 32 Geo. III, pt. 1 (C 66/3873) no. 1.

1792 8 Oct.

CORNWALLIS, M.
Charles Earl Cornwallis.
C 231/13, p. 92; 32 Geo. III, pt. 2 (C 66/3874) no. 14.

1793 22 May

AUCKLAND, B.
William Lord Auckland (I).
C 231/13, p. 105; 33 Geo. III, pt. 8 (C 66/3891)
no. 12 where dated 23 (*sic*) May.

1793 3 July

CARNARVON, E.
Henry Lord Porchester.
C 231/13, p. 108; 33 Geo. III, pt. 9 (C 66/3892) no. 9.

1793 5 July   **HERTFORD, M.**; Yarmouth, E.
Francis Earl of Hertford.
C 231/13, p. 109; 33 Geo. III, pt. 9 (C 66/3892) no. 7.

1794 9 Aug.   **UPPER OSSORY, B.**
John Earl of Upper Ossory (I).
C 231/13, p. 129; 34 Geo. III, pt. 11 (C 66/3904)
no. 14.

1794 13 Aug.   **CLIVE, B.**
Edward Lord Clive (I).
C 231/13, p. 129; 34 Geo. III, pt. 11 (C 66/3904)
no. 10.

1794 13 Aug.   **MULGRAVE, B.**
Henry Lord Mulgrave (I).
C 231/13, p. 129; 34 Geo. III, pt. 11 (C 66/3904)
no. 9.

1794 13 Aug.   **LYTTELTON, B.**
William Henry Lord Westcote (I).
C 231/13, p. 129; 34 Geo. III, pt. 11 (C 66/3904)
no. 8.

1794 13 Aug.   **MENDIP, B.**
Welbore Ellis.
Remainder, failing heirs male, to (1) Henry Welbore
Agar Viscount Clifden (I), (2) Hon. and Rev. John Ellis
Agar, (3) Hon. Charles Bagenal Agar, second and third
sons of James late Viscount Clifden (I), (4) Welbore Ellis
Agar, Commissioner of Customs, (5) Charles Agar,
Archbishop of Cashel and their heirs male respectively.
C 231/13, p. 129; 34 Geo. III, pt. 11 (C 66/3904)
no. 7.

1794 13 Aug.   **BRADFORD, B.**
Sir Henry Bridgeman, Bart.
C 231/13, p. 130; 34 Geo. III, pt. 11 (C 66/3904)
no. 6.

1794 13 Aug.   **SELSEY, B.**
Sir James Peachey, Bart.
C 231/13, p. 130; 34 Geo. III, pt. 11 (C 66/3904)
no. 5.

1794 13 Aug.   **DUNDAS, B.**
                    Sir Thomas Dundas, Bart.
                    C 231/13, p. 130; 34 Geo. III, pt. 11 (C 66/3904)
                    no. 4.

1794 13 Aug.   **CURZON, B.**
                    Assheton Curzon.
                    C 231/13, p. 130; 34 Geo. III, pt. 11 (C 66/3904)
                    no. 3.

1794 13 Aug.   **YARBOROUGH, B.**
                    Charles Anderson Pelham.
                    C 231/13, p. 130; 34 Geo. III, pt. 11 (C 66/3904)
                    no. 2.

1795 27 Mar.   **HOOD, B.**
                    Susanna Baroness Hood (I).
                    Remainder to heirs male by husband Samuel Lord
                    Hood (I).
                    C 231/13, p. 143; 35 Geo. III, pt. 5 (C 66/3911)
                    no. 11.

1795 31 Oct.   **LOUGHBOROUGH, B.**
                    Alexander Lord Loughborough.
                    Remainder, failing heirs male, to Sir James St. Clair
                    Erskine, Bart. and John Erskine his brother and their heirs
                    male respectively.
                    C 231/13, p. 153; 36 Geo. III, pt. 2 (C 66/3918)
                    no. 7.

1796 1 Mar.   **BUTE, M.;** Windsor, E.; Mountjoy, V.
                    John Earl of Bute (S) & Lord Mountstuart (GB).
                    C 231/13, p. 156; 36 Geo. III, pt. 5 (C 66/3921) no. 6;
                    dated 21 (*sic*) Mar. in *CP*, ii, 443.

1796 22 Apr.   **WARRINGTON, E.;** Delamer, B.
                    George Harry Earl of Stamford.
                    C 231/13, p. 163; 36 Geo. III, pt. 8 (C 66/3924)
                    no. 9.

1796 1 June   **LIVERPOOL, E.**
                    Charles Lord Hawkesbury.
                    C 231/13, p. 165; 36 Geo. III, pt. 11 (C 66/3927)
                    no. 22.

1796 1 June

HOOD, V.
Samuel Lord Hood (I).
C 231/13, p. 166; 36 Geo. III, pt. 11 (C 66/3927)
no. 23.

1796 4 June

STUART, B.
Francis Earl of Moray (S).
C 231/13, p. 166; 36 Geo. III, pt. 11 (C 66/3927)
no. 21.

1796 6 June

STEWART, B.
John Earl of Galloway (S).
C 231/13, p. 166; 36 Geo. III, pt. 11 (C 66/3927)
no. 20.

1796 7 June

SALTERSFORD, B.
James Earl of Courtown (I).
C 231/13, p. 166; 36 Geo. III, pt. 11 (C 66/3927)
no. 19.

1796 8 June

MACARTNEY, B.
George Earl of Macartney (I).
C 231/13, p. 167; 36 Geo. III, pt. 11 (C 66/3927)
no. 18.

1796 9 June

DAWNAY, B.
John Christopher Burton Viscount Downe (I).
C 231/13, p. 167; 36 Geo. III, pt. 11 (C 66/3927)
no. 13.

1796 11 June

BRODRICK, B.
George Viscount Midleton (I).
Remainder, failing heirs male, to heirs male of father
George Viscount Midleton (I).
C 231/13, p. 167; 36 Geo. III, pt. 11 (C 66/3927)
no. 11.

1796 13 June

BRIDPORT, B.
Alexander Lord Bridport (I).
C 231/13, p. 167; 36 Geo. III, pt. 11 (C 66/3927)
no. 10.

1796 14 June

ROUS, B.
Sir John Rous, Bart.
C 231/13, p. 168; 36 Geo. III, pt. 11 (C 66/3927)
no. 9.

1796 15 June   **CALTHORPE, B.**
Sir Henry Gough Calthorpe, Bart.
C 231/13, p. 168; 36 Geo. III, pt. 11 (C 66/3927)
no. 8; dated 16 (*sic*) June in *CP*, ii, 490.

1796 16 June   **GWYDIR, B.**
Sir Peter Burrell, Bart.
C 231/13, p. 168; 36 Geo. III, pt. 11 (C 66/3927)
no. 7.

1796 17 June   **DE DUNSTANVILLE, B.**
Sir Francis Basset, Bart.
C 231/13, p. 168; 36 Geo. III, pt. 11 (C 66/3927)
no. 6.

1796 18 June   **HAREWOOD, B.**
Edward Lascelles.
C 231/13, p. 168; 36 Geo. III, pt. 11 (C 66/3927)
no. 5.

1796 20 June   **ROLLE, B.**
John Rolle.
C 231/13, p. 168; 36 Geo. III, pt. 11 (C 66/3927)
no. 4.

1796 21 June   **CAWDOR, B.**
John Campbell.
C 231/13, p. 169; 36 Geo. III, pt. 11 (C 66/3927)
no. 1.

1796 23 July   **NEWARK, V.**; Pierrepont, B.
Charles Pierrepont.
C 231/13, p. 170; 36 Geo. III, pt. 13 (C 66/3929)
no. 5.

1797 23 June   **ST. VINCENT, E.**; Jervis, B.
Sir John Jervis, Kt.
C 231/13, p. 188; 37 Geo. III, pt. 9 (C 66/3939)
no. 2.

1797 20 Oct.   **WELLESLEY, B.**
Richard Earl of Mornington (I).
C 231/13, p. 193; LP 37 Geo. III enrolled 38 (*sic*) Geo.
III, pt. 1 (C 66/3943) no. 20.

1797 20 Oct.   **CARRINGTON, B.**
Robert Lord Carrington (I).
C 231/13, p. 193; LP 37 Geo. III enrolled 38 (*sic*)
Geo. III, pt. 1 (C 66/3943) no. 19.

1797 20 Oct.   **BAYNING, V.**
Charles Townshend.
C 231/13, p. 193; LP 37 Geo. III enrolled 38 (*sic*)
Geo. III, pt. 1 (C 66/3943) no. 18.

1797 20 Oct.   **GLASTONBURY, B.**
James Grenville.
Remainder, failing heirs male, to Lieutenant General
    Richard Grenville and heirs male.
C 231/13, p. 193; LP 37 Geo. III enrolled 38 (*sic*)
Geo. III, pt. 1 (C 66/3943) no. 22.

1797 20 Oct.   **BOLTON, B.**
Thomas Orde Powlett.
C 231/13, p. 193; LP 37 Geo. III enrolled 38 (*sic*)
Geo. III, pt. 1 (C 66/3943) no. 23.

1797 20 Oct.   **MINTO, B.**
Sir Gilbert Elliot Murray Kynynmound, Bart.
C 231/13, p. 193; LP 37 Geo. III enrolled 38 (*sic*)
Geo. III, pt. 1 (C 66/3943) no. 24.

1797 26 Oct.   **LOWTHER, V.**; Lowther, B.
James Earl of Lonsdale.
For life with remainder to heirs male of Sir William
Lowther, Bart. and heirs male.
C 231/13, p. 194; 38 Geo. III, pt. 1 (C 66/3943)
no. 17.

1797 26 Oct.   **WODEHOUSE, B.**
Sir John Wodehouse, Bart.
C 231/13, p. 194; 38 Geo. III, pt. 1 (C 66/3943)
no. 16.

1797 26 Oct.   **NORTHWICK, B.**
Sir John Rushout, Bart.
C 231/13, p. 194; 38 Geo. III, pt. 1 (C 66/3943)
no. 15.

1797 26 Oct.

LILFORD, B.
Thomas Powys.
C 231/13, p. 194; 38 Geo. III, pt. 1 (C 66/3943)
no. 14.

1797 26 Oct.

RIBBLESDALE, B.
Thomas Lister.
C 231/13, p. 194; 38 Geo. III, pt. 1 (C 66/3943)
no. 13.

1797 26 Oct.

PERTH, B.
James Drummond.
C 231/13, p. 194; 38 Geo. III, pt. 1 (C 66/3943)
no. 12.

1797 26 Oct.

SEAFORTH, B.
Francis Humberstone MacKenzie.
C 231/13, p. 194; 38 Geo. III, pt. 1 (C 66/3943)
no. 11.

1797 30 Oct.

DUNCAN, V.; Duncan, B.
Adam Duncan.
C 231/13, p. 195; 38 Geo. III, pt. 1 (C 66/3943)
no. 10.

1797 30 Nov.

BASSET, B.
Francis Lord de Dunstanville.
Remainder, failing heirs male, to daughter Frances and
heirs male.
C 231/13, p. 197; 38 Geo. III, pt. 2 (C 66/3944)
no. 22.

1798 6 Nov.

NELSON, B.
Sir Horatio Nelson, Kt.
C 231/13, p. 214; 39 Geo. III, pt. 1 (C 66/3952) no. 8.

1799 24 Apr.

KENT & STRATHEARN, D.; Dublin, E. (I)
Prince Edward.
C 231/13, p. 221; 39 Geo. III, pt. 7 (C 66/3958)
no. 3.

1799 24 Apr.

CUMBERLAND & TEVIOTDALE, D.; Armagh, E. (I)
Prince Ernest Augustus.
C 231/13, p. 221; 39 Geo. III, pt. 7 (C 66/3958) no. 2.

1799 18 July

ELDON, B.
Sir John Scott, Kt.
C 231/13, p. 230; 39 Geo. III, pt. 11 (C 66/3962) no. 18.

1799 24 Sept.

FITZGIBBON, B.
John Earl of Clare (I).
C 231/13, p. 231; 39 Geo. III, pt. 11 (C 66/3962) no. 1.

1800 16 June

BRIDPORT, V.
Alexander Lord Bridport (I & GB).
C 231/13, p. 248; 40 Geo. III, pt. 11 (C 66/3973) no. 6.

1800 27 Dec.

CADOGAN, E.; Chelsea, V.
Charles Sloane Lord Cadogan.
C 231/13, p. 285; 41 Geo. III, pt. 4 (C 66/3982) no. 2.

1800 29 Dec.

MALMESBURY, E.; Fitzharris, V.
James Lord Malmesbury.
C 231/13, p. 285; 41 Geo. III, pt. 4 (C 66/3982) no. 1.

Creations by Protector Oliver

1657 20 July   **HOWARD, V.**; Dacre, B.
                                 Charles Howard.
                                 C 231/6, p. 373.

1658 26 Apr.   **BURNELL, B.**
                                 Edmund Dunch.
                                 C 231/6, p. 391.

Irish Peerage Creations
1603–1898

A Chronological List of Creations
in the Peerage of Ireland

ABBREVIATIONS

B.	Barony
Bart.	Baronet
Chas.	Charles
D.	Dukedom
E.	Earldom
(E)	Peerage of England
(GB)	Peerage of Great Britain
Geo.	George
Jas.	James
Kt.	Knight
LP	Letters patent
M.	Marquessate
(S)	Peerage of Scotland
(UK)	Peerage of United Kingdom
V.	Viscountcy
Will.	William

REFERENCES

Manuscript

The National Archives, London

C 66   Chancery: Patent Rolls

C 231   Chancery: Crown Office Docket Books 1615–43, 1660–1810

Printed works

Abstract   *Abstract of the Patent and Miscellaneous Rolls of Chancery 1830–37*, comp. G. Hatchell (Dublin, 1838).

Calendar   *Irish Patent Rolls of James: Facsimile of the Irish Record Commission's Calendar* (Dublin, 1966).

Claims to Vote   *Claims to vote at elections for representative peers: minutes of evidence taken before the committee for privileges* (House of Lords Record Office, 4 vols, Various dates).

CP   *Complete Peerage*, ed. G.E.C. (2nd edn, 14 vols, 1910–98).

List   'Mr Le Bas' List of all the patentees of . . . titles . . . 1795–1817', in *Liber Munerum Publicorum Hiberniae, or the Establishments of Ireland*, being the Report of R. Lascelles, vol. 1, part III.

LJ   *Lords Journals*

LJI   *Lords Journals (Ireland)*

Lodge   J. Lodge, *The Peerage of Ireland: or, a genealogical history of the present nobility of that kingdom*, revised and continued to the present time by M. Archdall. (6 vols., 1789).

Peerage   'The Peerage of Ireland', in *Liber Munerum Publicorum Hiberniae, or the Establishments of Ireland*, being the Report of R. Lascelles, vol. 1, part I.

Introduction

In 1998 the Parliamentary History Yearbook Trust published *Peerage Creations 1649–1800* (a revised edition is to be found above 1–67). This provided a list of creations in the peerages of England and Great Britain between those years arranged chronologically. The opportunity was taken to correct errors that had found their way into standard secondary sources.

The present work extends the same approach to creations in the peerage of Ireland, listing them from the accession of James I in 1603 until the last such creation which took place in 1898. It thus includes creations both of peers of the old kingdom of Ireland and also of those peers created under the special provisions of the Act of Union of 1800.[1]

Peerages of Ireland, like those of England, were created by letters patent. Until the establishment of Great Britain in 1707 such letters patent might be passed under the great seals of either England or Ireland. Thereafter the great seal of Ireland was invariably adopted for this purpose except in the limited case of members of the royal family whose Irish earldoms were conferred by the same letters patent as their British dukedoms.[2]

The principal sources for letters patent of creation passed under the great seals of England and Great Britain are twofold: the crown office docket books and the patent rolls preserved in the National Archives (Public Record Office). The docket books record in chronological sequence the issue of certain documents passed under the great seal including grants of peerages. The docket books minute the date and contents of each patent in summary form.

The docket books for the years 1603–15 and for the period of Charles II's exile 1649–60 are missing. Otherwise the sequence is complete.[3] As a general rule the full texts of patents themselves are enrolled on the patent rolls.[4]

Whereas for creations made under the great seal of England it is possible to attain precision of dating in almost every instance, the position is far otherwise in the case of those passed under the great seal of Ireland due to the destruction of the patent rolls along with the rest of the public records of Ireland in 1922. By this date the process of calendaring the rolls had not progressed beyond the years 1603–29 and 1830–37.[5]

---

[1] For the peerage of Ireland generally, see earl of Halsbury, *The Laws of England* (31 vols, 1907–17), xxii, 267–9; M.F. Bond, *Guide to the Records of Parliament* (1971), p. 167.

[2] The earldoms in question were those of Ulster (1716, 1760 and 1784), Connaught (1764), Dublin (1766 and 1799), Munster (1789), Armagh (1799).

[3] C 231/3–5, 7–13.

[4] C 66.

[5] *Irish Patent Rolls of James I; Facsimile of the Irish Record Commission's Calendar* (Dublin, 1966); J. Morris, *Calendar of the Patent and Close Rolls of Chancery in Ireland, of the Reign of Charles the First. First to eighth year, inclusive.* Dublin, 1863; *Abstract of the Patent and Close Rolls of Chancery 1830–37*, comp. G. Hatchell (Dublin, 1838).

Given this state of affairs the relevant information has for the most part to be sought elsewhere. The principal source is the material collected in volume 1 of the *Liber Munerum*.[6] Three sections of this work are of relevance, the first two of which are paginated consecutively and entitled 'The Peerage of Ireland'[7]:

(1) lists of peerage creations arranged chronologically by rank from the earliest times to 1785. Up to 1771 this was compiled by John Lodge (d. 1774), the author of a peerage of Ireland published in 1754[8] whose office of deputy keeper of the records in the Bermingham Tower in Dublin gave him ready access to the relevant documentation. These lists are continued, less reliably, 'from Archdall' to 1785. Mervyn Archdall (d. 1791) was the author of a revised edition of Lodge's peerage published in 1789;[9]

(2) extracts from the *Journals* of the Irish house of lords 1753–1800 providing details of the occasions when peers took their seats in the House including dates of letters patent in the case of peers of first creation.[10] While these extracts are of particular assistance for the period between the cessation of the Archdall list in 1785 and the abolition of the House in 1800 they are obviously of no value for the creations of those who never took their seats in the House;

(3) 'Mr Le Bas' List', compiled by a clerk in the office of chief secretary for Ireland, which provides the dates of instruments, including peerage creations, which passed under the great seal of Ireland between 1795 and 1817.[11]

The information provided by the *Liber Munerum* can be supplemented by reference to the printed *Journals* of the Irish and English houses of lords. In the former are printed the full texts of 18 17th century Irish peerage patents.[12] Following the Union in 1801 those peers wishing to vote at elections for Irish representative peers were required to submit their claims to the House for verification. Some of the relevant petitions printed in the *Journals* contain details of dates of creation. On occasion the minutes of evidence and the reports made to the House on the claims contain printed texts of the letters patent. The original letters patent creating the barony of Kiltarton (1810) survive in the parchment collection of the Parliamentary Archives.

Where no other documentation is available the *Complete Peerage* has been consulted. This work has to be treated with some caution since, in the absence of references, it is often impossible to discover on what sources that work was relying.

In summary the list is designed to provide the following information:

[6] *Liber Munerum Publicorum Hiberniae, or the Establishments of Ireland*, being the Report of R. Lascelles (2 vols, Ordered to be printed 1824).

[7] *Liber Munerum*, vol. 1, pt. i, pp. 1–52.

[8] J. Lodge, *The Peerage of Ireland, or, a Genealogical History of the Present Nobility of that Kingdom* (4 vols, 1754).

[9] J. Lodge, *The Peerage of Ireland . . .*, revised and continued to the present time by M. Archdall (6 vols, 1789).

[10] *Liber Munerum*, vol. 1, pt. i, pp. 53–69.

[11] *Liber Munerum*, vol. 1, pt. iii, pp. 52a–u.

[12] *LJI*, i, 74–97, 188.

1. The date of creation. The year is taken to have begun on 1 January throughout.
2. The principal title conferred (capitalised), followed by any other titles in descending order of rank. For the spelling of titles the usage of the *Complete Peerage* has been adopted.
3. The name of the grantee. Grantees who were peers should be understood to be peers of Ireland unless otherwise specified.
4. In cases where the peerage was for life this fact is noted; similarly those cases where the remainder was other than to heirs male of the body. In the list the term 'heirs male' should be construed as 'heirs male of the body.'
5. The sources from which the information is derived. Where available the references to the *Liber Munerum* are noted. In the case of letters patent passed under the great seal of England or Great Britain, the reference to the docket book is followed by a reference to the enrolment on the patent roll. Where the text of the letters patent is available in print the fact is noted. In addition the opportunity has been taken to note those frequent instances in which Lodge printed the preambles to letters patent. Where dates of creation recorded in the *Complete Peerage* or other published sources differ from those given in the text the fact is noted.

Creations 1603–1898

James I

1603 13 July   **ORMOND AND OSSORY, E.**
Theobald Butler.
Reversion after death of present earl without male issue to self and heirs male; failing whom to heirs male of great grandfather Peter Butler.
Peerage, p. 5; LP 1 Jas. I, pt. 6 (C 66/1612) no. 38.

1603 4 Aug.   **BUTLER, V.**
Theobald Butler.
Peerage, p. 19; LP 1 Jas. I, pt. 4 (C 66/1610).

1603 27 Sept.   **TYRCONNEL, E.**
Roderick O'Donnell.
Remainder, failing heirs male, to brother Geoffrey O'Donnell and heirs male.
Peerage, p. 5.

1613 23 Feb.   **CHICHESTER, B.**
Sir Arthur Chichester, Kt.
Peerage, p. 38; LP 10 Jas. I, pt. 1 (C 66/1943) no. 16; preamble printed in Lodge, i, 323–4.

1616 25 May   **RIDGEWAY, B.**
Sir Thomas Ridgeway, Bart.
Peerage, p. 38.

1616 19 July   **BRABAZON, B.**
Sir Edward Brabazon, Kt.
Peerage, p. 38; preamble printed in Lodge, i, 272–3.

1616 20 July   **MOORE, B.**
Sir Gerald Moore, Kt.
Peerage, p. 38; preamble printed in Lodge, ii, 95–6.

1616 6 Sept.

CASTLEHAVEN, E.; Audley, B.
George Baron Audley (E).
Peerage, p. 5.

1616 6 Sept.

BOYLE, B.
Sir Richard Boyle, Kt.
Peerage, p. 38; *Calendar*, p. 304; dated 6 May (*sic*) 1616
in *CP*, iii, 419–20; preamble printed in Lodge, i, 156–7.

1617 8 May

HAMILTON, B.
Hon. James Hamilton.
Remainder, failing heirs male, to heirs male of father.
Peerage, p. 38; preamble printed in Lodge, v, 112–13.

1618 31 Jan.

MOUNTJOY, B.
Mountjoy Blount.
Peerage, p. 38.

1618 17 Feb.

LAMBART, B.
Sir Oliver Lambart, Kt.
Peerage, p. 38; preamble printed in Lodge, i, 351.

1618 17 Feb.

BOURKE, B.
Theobald Bourke.
Peerage, p. 38.

1618 26 June

DUNLUCE, V.
Sir Randal M'Donnell, Kt.
Calendar, p. 373; dated 28 May (*sic*) 1618 in *CP*, i, 174
and 25 (*sic*) June 1618 in *Peerage*, p. 19; preamble printed
in Lodge, i, 205–06.

1619 19 Feb.

POWERSCOURT, V.
Sir Richard Wingfield, Kt.
Peerage, p. 19; *Calendar*, pp. 412–13; dated 19 Feb. 1618
(*sic*) in *CP*, x, 636; preamble printed in Lodge, v, 271.

1619 11 July

DESMOND, E.; Dunmore, B.
Richard Lord Dingwall (S).
C 231/4 f. 90; *CP*, iv, 257; dated 11 or 24 (*sic*) July
1619 in *Peerage*, p. 5.

1619 7 Nov.

CASTLE STEWART, B.
Andrew Stewart.
Peerage, p. 38.

1619 8 Nov.   **BALFOUR, B.**
Sir James Balfour, Kt.
Peerage, p. 38.

1620 22 Jan.   **FOLLIOTT, B.**
Sir Henry Folliott, Kt.
Peerage, p. 38.

1620 24 Jan.   **DILLON, B.**
Sir James Dillon, Kt.
Peerage, p. 39; preamble printed in Lodge, iv, 158.

1620 30 May   **MAYNARD, B.**
Sir William Maynard, Bart.
Peerage, p. 39; C 231/4 f. 106; LP 18 Jas. I, pt. 18
(C 66/2233) no. 1.

1620 13 July   **GORGES, B.**
Sir Edward Gorges, Bart.
Peerage, p. 39; C 231/4 f. 110v; LP 18 Jas. I, pt. 14
(C 66/2229) no. 20.

1620 29 July   **DIGBY, B.**
Sir Robert Digby, Kt.
Remainder, failing heirs male, to brothers and heirs
male.
Peerage, p. 39; preamble printed in Lodge, vi, 289.

1620 5 Aug.   **HERVEY, B.**
Sir William Hervey, Bart.
Remainder to son William Hervey and heirs male;
failing whom to heirs male of self hereafter to be
begotten.
Peerage, p. 39; C 231/4 f. 112; LP 18 Jas. I, pt. 10
(C 66/2225) no. 13.

1620 16 Oct.   **CORK, E.**; Dungarvan, V.
Richard Baron Boyle.
C 231/4 f. 113v; *CP*, iii, 420; LP 18 Jas. I, pt. 5
(C 66/2220) no. 10; dated 26 (*sic*) Oct. 1620 in *Peerage*,
p. 5.

1620 1 Dec.   **FITZWILLIAM, B.**
William Fitzwilliam.
Peerage, p. 39; C 231/4 f. 113v; LP 18 Jas. I, pt. 6
(C 66/2221) no. 9.

1620 12 Dec.   **ANTRIM, E.**
Randal Viscount Dunluce.
Peerage, p. 6; C 231/4 f. 116; LP 18 Jas. I, pt. 6
(C 66/2221) no. 4; preamble printed in Lodge, i, 206.

1620 22 Dec.   **CAULFIELD, B.**
Sir Toby Caulfield, Kt.
Remainder, failing heirs male, to nephew Sir William
Caulfield and heirs male.
Peerage, p. 39; preamble printed in Lodge, iii, 130–33.

1621 3 Jan.   **GRANDISON, V.**
Sir Oliver St. John, Kt.
Remainder, failing heirs male, to heirs male of niece
Barbara wife of Sir Edward Villiers, Kt.
Peerage, p. 20; C 231/4 f. 116v; LP 18 Jas. I, pt. 16
(C 66/2231) no. 19 printed in *Claims to Vote*, iii, 27–31.

1621 4 Jan.   **WILMOT, V.**
Sir Charles Wilmot, Kt.
Peerage, p. 20; C 231/4 f. 116v; LP 18 Jas. I, pt. 16
(C 66/2231) no. 21.

1621 1 Mar.   **VALENTIA, V.**
Sir Henry Power, Kt.
Peerage, p. 20; C 231/4 f. 120v; LP 18 Jas. I, pt. 12
(C 66/2227) no. 16.

1621 25 May   **DOCKWRA, B.**
Sir Henry Dockwra, Kt.
C 231/4 f. 124; *CP*, iv, 387; LP 19 Jas. I, pt. 13
(C 66/2257) no. 17; dated 15 (*sic*) May 1621 in *Peerage*,
p. 39.

1621 29 June   **AUNGIER, B.**
Sir Francis Aungier, Kt.
Peerage, p. 39; C 231/4 f. 125v; LP 19 Jas. I, pt. 11
(C 66/2255) no. 5; preamble printed in Lodge, iii, 376–7.

1621 13 July   **VAUGHAN, B.**
Sir John Vaughan, Kt.
Peerage, p. 39; C 231/4 f. 127; LP 19 Jas. I, pt. 6
(C 66/2250) no. 15.

1621 29 July   **BLAYNEY, B.**
                    Sir Edward Blayney, Kt.
                    Peerage, p. 39; LP printed in *LJI*, i, 86.

1621 4 Sept.   **WESTMEATH, E.**
                    Richard Baron Delvin.
                    Peerage, p. 6; C 231/4 f. 128v; LP 19 Jas. I, pt. 9
                    (C 66/2249) no. 16 printed in *LJI*, i, 75–6.

1622 7 Feb.   **MOORE, V.**
                    Gerald Baron Moore.
                    Peerage, p. 20; preamble printed in Lodge, ii, 97.

1622 11 Mar.   **VALENTIA, V.**
                    Sir Francis Annesley, Bart.
                    Reversion after death of present viscount without heirs
                    male to self and heirs male.
                    Peerage, p. 20; C 231/4 f. 136v; LP 19 Jas. I, pt. 9
                    (C 66/2253) no. 8.

1622 16 Mar.   **DILLON, V.**
                    Sir Theobald Dillon, Kt.
                    Peerage, p. 20; C 231/4 f. 136v; LP 19 Jas. I, pt. 9
                    (C 66/2253) no. 2; preamble printed in Lodge, iv,
                    177–8.

1622 3 Apr.   **NETTERVILLE, V.**
                    Nicholas Netterville.
                    Peerage, p. 20; C 231/4 f. 137v; LP 20 Jas. I, pt. 11
                    (C 66/2279) no. 21 printed in *LJI*, i, 83.

1622 3 May   **MONTGOMERY, V.**
                    Sir Hugh Montgomery, Kt.
                    Peerage, p. 21; C 231/4 f. 138; LP 20 Jas. I, pt. 10
                    (C 66/2278) no. 4.

1622 4 May   **CLANEBOYE, V.**
                    Sir James Hamilton, Kt.
                    Peerage, p. 21; C 231/4 f. 138v; LP 20 Jas. I, pt. 10
                    (C 66/2278) no. 3; preamble printed in Lodge, iii, 3.

1622 10 May   **LOFTUS, V.**
                    Sir Adam Loftus, Kt.
                    Peerage, p. 21; LP printed in *LJI*, i, 74–5.

1622 20 May   **BEAUMONT, V.**
Sir Thomas Beaumont, Bart.
Peerage, p. 21.

1622 20 May   **ESMOND, B.**
Sir Laurence Esmond, Kt.
Peerage, p. 39; LP printed in *LJI*, i, 88.

1622 5 Aug.   **ROSCOMMON, E.**
James Baron Dillon.
Peerage, p. 6; preamble printed in Lodge, iv, 158–9.

1622 23 Aug.   **LONDONDERRY, E.**
Thomas Baron Ridgeway.
Peerage, p. 6.

1622 5 Oct.   **GLEAN O'MALLUN, B.**
Sir Dermot O'Mallun, Kt.
For life with remainder to elder son Albert and heirs male failing whom to younger son Francis and heirs male.
C 231/4 f. 145; LP 20 Jas. I, pt. 3 (C 66/2271) no. 33; dated 1 (*sic*) Oct. 1622 in *Peerage*, p. 39.

1622 7 Nov.   **CALLAN, V.**; Feilding, B.
DESMOND, E.
Hon. George Feilding.
For viscountcy and barony remainder to heirs male; for earldom reversion after death of present earl without heirs male to self with remainder to heirs male.
C 231/4 f. 146v; *CP*, ii, 487; LP 20 Jas. I, pt. 1 (C 66/2269), no. 19; dated 22 (*sic*) Nov. 1622 in *Peerage*, p. 6.

1623 18 July   **MAGENNIS, V.**
Sir Arthur Magennis, Kt.
Peerage, p. 21; C 231/4 f. 155v; LP 21 Jas. I, pt. 6 (C 66/2300) no. 10 printed in *LJI*, i, 95.

1624 11 May   **BRERETON, B.**
Sir William Brereton, Kt.
Peerage, p. 39; C 231/4 f. 164v; LP 22 Jas. I, pt. 17 (C 66/2340) no. 7.

1624 12 Nov.

LECALE, V.
Thomas Baron Cromwell (E).
Peerage, p. 22; LP printed in *LJI*, i, 89; dated 22 (*sic*)
Nov. 1624 in *CP*, i, 192.

1624 31 Dec.

HERBERT, B.
Sir Edward Herbert, Kt.
C 231/4 f. 174; *CP*, vi, 441; LP 22 Jas. I, pt. 15
(C 66/2338) no. 7; dated 30 (*sic*) Dec. 1624 in *Peerage*,
p. 39.

1625 16 Feb.

BALTIMORE, B.
Sir George Calvert, Kt.
Peerage, p. 39; C 231/4 f. 176; LP 22 Jas. I, pt. 16
(C 66/2339) no. 5.

Charles I

1625 1 Apr.

CHICHESTER, V.; Chichester, B.
Sir Edward Chichester, Kt.
Peerage, p. 22; C 231/4 f. 181v; LP 1 Chas. I, pt. 3
(C 66/2350) no. 18; preamble printed in Lodge, i, 328–9.

1625 8 Apr.

KILMOREY, V.
Sir Robert Needham, Kt.
C 231/4 f. 183v; *CP*, vii, 260; LP 1 Chas. I, pt. 3
(C 66/2350) no. 15 printed in *Claims to Vote*, iii, 191–2;
dated 18 (*sic*) Apr. 1625 in *Peerage*, p. 22.

1625 8 May

KINSALE, V.; Barretts Country, B.
Sir Dominick Sarsfield, Bart.
Peerage, p. 22.

1625 31 Aug.

COLERAINE, B.
Hugh Hare.
Peerage, p. 39; C 231/4 f. 192v; LP 1 Chas. I, pt. 9
(C 66/2356) no. 6.

1626 8 Dec.

SOMERSET, V.
Sir Thomas Somerset, Kt.
Peerage, p. 22; C 231/4 f. 212v; LP 2 Chas. I, pt. 5
(C 66/2377) no. 10.

1627 15 Mar. **KILLULTAGH, V.**
Edward Baron Conway (E).
Peerage, p. 22; C 231/4 f. 220; LP 2 Chas. I, pt. 5
(C 66/2377) no. 13.

1627 16 Apr. **MEATH, E.**
William Baron Brabazon.
Remainder, failing heirs male, to brother Sir Anthony
Brabazon, Kt. and heirs male.
Peerage, p. 7; LP printed in *LJI*, i, 76–7.

1627 21 June **MAYO, V.**
Sir Theobald Bourke, Kt.
Peerage, p. 22; LP printed in *LJI*, i, 97.

1627 27 June **BALTINGLASS, V.**; Bantry, B.
Sir Thomas Roper, Kt.
Peerage, p. 23.

1627 10 July **SHERARD, B.**
Sir William Sherard, Kt.
Peerage, p. 39; C 231/4 f. 230v; LP 3 Chas. I, pt. 6
(C 66/2412) no. 15.

1627 11 July **CASTLETON, V.**; Saunderson, B.
Sir Nicholas Saunderson, Bart.
Peerage, p. 23; C 231/4 f. 231; LP 3 Chas. I, pt. 6
(C 66/2412) no. 17.

1627 17 Sept. **SARSFIELD, V.**
Dominick Viscount Kinsale.
Peerage, p. 22.

1628 28 Feb. **BARRYMORE, E.**
David Viscount Buttevant.
Peerage, p. 7; preamble printed in Lodge, i, 296.

1628 28 Feb. **BOYLE, V.**; Bandon Bridge, B.
Hon. Lewis Boyle.
Remainder, failing heirs male, to heirs male of father,
failing whom to heirs male for ever.
Peerage, p. 23; LP printed in H. Nicolas, *Report on
Claim to Earldom of Devon* (1832), Appendix, pp. lv–lx.

1628 28 Feb.   **BROGHILL, B.**
                        Hon. Roger Boyle.
                        Remainder, failing heirs male, to heirs male of father,
                        failing whom to heirs male for ever.
                        Peerage, p. 40; LP printed in H. Nicolas, *Report on
                        Claim to Earldom of Devon* (1832), Appendix, pp. lx–lxii.

1628 3 Mar.   **MAGUIRE, B.**
                        Sir Bryan Roe Maguire, Kt.
                        Peerage, p. 40.

1628 4 Mar.   **CHAWORTH, V.**; Chaworth, B.
                        Sir George Chaworth, Kt.
                        Peerage, p. 23; C 231/4 f. 241; LP 3 Chas. I, pt. 11
                        (C 66/2417) no. 7.

1628 21 Mar.   **CARLINGFORD, V.**
                        Barnham Swift.
                        C 231/4 f. 243; LP 3 Chas. I, pt. 6 (C 66/2412)
                        no. 12; dated 20 (*sic*) Mar. 1628 in *Peerage*, p. 23.

1628 11 June   **SAVILE, V.**; Castelbar, B.
                        Hon. Sir Thomas Savile, Kt.
                        Peerage, p. 23.

1628 1 July   **SCUDAMORE, V.**; Dromore, B.
                        Sir John Scudamore, Bart.
                        Peerage, p. 23; C 231/4 f. 248; *CP*, xi, 573; dated 2 (*sic*)
                        July 1628 in LP 4 Chas. I, pt. 39 (C 66/2494) no. 27.

1628 2 July   **CHOLMONDELEY, V**.
                        Sir Robert Cholmondeley, Bart.
                        Peerage, p. 23; C 231/4 f. 248v; LP 4 Chas. I, pt. 39
                        (C 66/2494) no. 25.

1628 12 July   **LUMLEY, V.**
                        Sir Richard Lumley, Kt.
                        Peerage, p. 23; C 231/4 f. 250v; LP 4 Chas. I, pt. 39
                        (C 66/2494) no. 23.

1628 17 July   **STRANGFORD, V.**
                        Sir Thomas Smythe, Kt.
                        Peerage, p. 24; C 231/4 f. 251; LP 4 Chas. I, pt. 39
                        (C 66/2494) no. 17.

1628 30 July

WENMAN, V.; Wenman, B.
Sir Richard Wenman, Kt.
Peerage, p. 24; C 231/4 f. 252v; LP 4 Chas. I, pt. 39
(C 66/2494) no. 28; preamble printed in Lodge, iv,
282–3.

1628 1 Aug.

TAAFFE, V.; Ballymote, B.
Sir John Taaffe, Kt.
Peerage, p. 24; LP printed in *LJI*, i, 79–80.

1628 5 Aug.

CARBERY, E.
John Baron Vaughan.
Peerage, p. 7; C 231/4 f. 253v; LP 4 Chas. I, pt. 39
(C 66/2494) no. 12.

1628 23 Aug.

MONSON, V.; Monson, B.
Sir William Monson, Kt.
Peerage, p. 24; C 231/4 f. 254v; LP 4 Chas. I, pt. 28
(C 66/2477) no. 52.

1628 23 Aug.

GALWAY, V.; Immaney, B.
Richard Earl of Clanricarde (I) and Viscount
Tonbridge (E).
Remainder, failing heirs male, to heirs male of father.
Also grant of earldom of St. Albans (E).
Peerage, p. 24; C 231/4 f. 254v; LP 4 Chas. I, pt. 39
(C 66/2494) no. 20.

1628 25 Aug.

RANELAGH, V.; Navan, B.
Sir Roger Jones, Kt.
Peerage, p. 24; LP printed in *LJI*, i, 81–2.

1628 26 Sept.

FINGALL, E.
Luke Baron Killeen.
Peerage, p. 7; LP printed in *LJI*, i, 78.

1628 16 Oct.

DOWNE, E.; Pope, B.
Sir William Pope, Bart.
Peerage, p. 7; LP 4 Chas. I, pt. 39 (C 66/2494) no. 21;
dated 15 (*sic*) Oct. 1628 in C 231/4 f. 257v.

1628 15 Nov.   **MUSKERRY, V.**; Blarney, B.
Sir Charles Macarthy, Kt.
Remainder to son Donough and heirs male; failing whom to heirs male.
Peerage, p. 24.

1628 22 Dec.   **MOLYNEUX, V.**
Sir Richard Molyneux, Bart.
Peerage, p. 24; C 231/4 f. 262; LP 4 Chas. I, pt. 3 (C 66/2452) no. 38.

1629 8 Feb.   **MOUNTNORRIS, B**.
Sir Francis Annesley, Bart.
Peerage, p. 40; preamble printed in Lodge, iv, 114.

1629 10 Feb.   **FAIRFAX, V**.
Sir Thomas Fairfax, Kt.
Peerage, p. 24; C 231/4 f. 264; dated 10 Jan. (*sic*) 1629 in LP 4 Chas. I, pt. 8 (C 66/2457) no. 1 and *CP*, v, 234.

1629 20 Apr.   **BOURKE, V.**
Hon. John Bourke.
Remainder, failing heirs male, to heirs male of father.
Peerage, p. 24.

1629 12 May   **IKERRIN, V.**
Sir Pierce Butler, Kt.
Peerage, p. 24; LP printed in *LJI*, i, 80.

1629 5 Aug.   **FITZWILLIAM, V.**; Fitzwilliam, B.
Sir Thomas Fitzwilliam, Kt.
Peerage, p. 24; C 231/5 p. 16; LP 5 Chas. I, pt. 3 (C 66/2499) no. 8 printed in *LJI*, i, 87.

1631 22 Dec.   **CLANMALIER, V.**; Philipstown, B.
Sir Terence O'Dempsie, Kt.
Peerage, p. 25; LP printed in *LJI*, i, 85–6.

1634 14 Aug.   **HAMILTON, B.**
Hon. Claud Hamilton.
Remainder, failing heirs male, to heirs male of father.
Peerage, p. 38.

1642 28 July   **ALINGTON, B.**
William Alington.
Peerage, p. 40; C 231/5 p. 533.

1642 11 Aug.   **CULLEN, V.**; Cullen, B.
Charles Cokayne.
Remainder, failing heirs male, to Peregrine, Richard,
Vere and Charles Bertie and heirs male.
Peerage, p. 25; C 231/5 p. 535.

1642 30 Aug.   **ORMOND, M.**
James Earl of Ormond.
Peerage, p. 3; C 231/5 p. 537; LP printed in *LJI*, i, 188.

1643 12 Jan.   **TRACY, V.**; Tracy, B.
Sir John Tracy, Kt.
Peerage, p. 25; C 231/5 p. 544; LP 18 Chas. I, pt. 2
(C 66/2901) no. 7.

1643 4 Nov.   **CARRINGTON, V.**
Charles Baron Carrington (E).
Peerage, p. 25; C 231/3 p. 50.

1644 6 Jan.   **BULKELEY, V.**
Thomas Bulkeley.
Peerage, p. 25; C 231/3 p. 65; preamble printed in
Lodge, v, 26.

1645 26 Jan.   **ANTRIM, M.**
Randal Earl of Antrim.
Peerage, p. 3; C 231/3 p. 141; preamble printed in
Lodge, i, 206.

1645 15 Apr.   **ARDGLASS, E.**
Thomas Viscount Lecale and Baron Cromwell (E).
Peerage, p. 7.

1645 8 July   **HAWLEY, B.**
Sir Francis Hawley, Bart.
Peerage, p. 40; C 231/3 p. 156.

1645 18 July   **BELLOMONT, V.**; Bard, B.
Sir Henry Bard, Bart.
Peerage, p. 25; C 231/3 p. 156.

1645 7 Sept.

BROUNCKER, V.; Brouncker, B.
Sir William Brouncker, Kt.
C 231/3 p. 157; dated 12 (*sic*) Sept. 1645 in *Peerage*, p. 25 and *CP*, ii, 345.

1645 23 Dec.

OGLE, V.
Sir William Ogle, Kt.
Peerage, p. 25; C 231/3 p. 163.

1646 21 Feb.

CLANRICARDE, M.
Ulick Earl of Clanricarde and Earl of St. Albans (E).
C 231/3 p. 164; *CP*, iii, 231; dated 21 Feb. 1644 (*sic*) in *Peerage*, p. 3.

1646 5 Mar.

LEINSTER, E.
Robert Viscount Cholmondeley and Baron Cholmondeley (E).
Peerage, p. 7; C 231/3 p. 165.

1646 16 May

GALMOYE, V.
Sir Edward Butler, Kt.
Peerage, p. 25.

1646 29 June

BARNEWALL, V.; Turvey, B.
Nicholas Barnewall.
Peerage, p. 25; preamble printed in Lodge, v, 49.

1647 30 Mar.

DONEGALL, E.
Hon. Arthur Chichester.
Remainder, failing heirs male, to heirs male of father.
Peerage, p. 7; preamble printed in Lodge, i, 334.

1647 1 Apr.

CAVAN, E.; Kilcoursie, V.
Charles Baron Lambart.
Peerage, p. 7.

1647 7 June

CLANBRASSIL, E.
James Viscount Claneboye.
Peerage, p. 7; preamble printed in Lodge, iii, 4.

Charles II

1650 2 July   **TARA, V.**
Hon. Thomas Preston.
Peerage, p. 25.

1654 21 Oct.   **INCHIQUIN, E.**; O'Brien, B.
Murrough Baron Inchiquin.
Peerage, p. 7; LP printed in *Claims to Vote*, iii,
61–2.

1658 27 Nov.   **CLANCARTY, E.**
Donough Viscount Muskerry.
Peerage, p. 7.

1659 10 May   **ULSTER, E.**
James Duke of York (E).
CP, xii(2), 915.

1660 4 Sept.   **KINGSTON, B.**
Sir John King, Kt.
Peerage, p. 40; C 231/7 p. 37; LP 12 Chas. II, pt. 10
(C 66/2925) no. 9; preamble printed in Lodge, iii, 226–7.

1660 5 Sept.   **ORRERY, E.**
Roger Baron Broghill.
Peerage, p. 9; C 231/7 p. 37; preamble printed in Lodge,
i, 187.

1660 6 Sept.   **MOUNTRATH, E.**; Coote, V.; Coote, B.
Sir Charles Coote, Bart.
Peerage, p. 9; C 231/7 p. 37; LP 12 Chas. II, pt. 10
(C 66/2925) no. 10; preamble printed in Lodge, ii, 76.

1660 6 Sept.   **SHANNON, V.**
Hon. Francis Boyle.
Peerage, p. 25.

1660 6 Sept.   **COLOONY, B.**
Richard Coote.
Peerage, p. 40; C 231/7 p. 37; LP 12 Chas. II, pt. 10
(C 66/2925) no. 11; preamble printed in Lodge, iii,
203–04.

1660 21 Nov.

MASSEREENE, V.; Loughneagh, B.

Sir John Clotworthy, Kt.

Remainder, failing heirs male, to Sir John Skeffington, Kt. and heirs male by wife Mary, failing whom to heirs general.

Peerage, p. 25; C 231/7 p. 55; LP 12 Chas. II, pt. 11 (C 66/2926) no. 1; preamble printed in Lodge, ii, 378.

1661 18 Feb.

SANTRY, B.

Sir James Barry, Kt.

Peerage, p. 40; preamble printed in Lodge, i, 307.

1661 2 Mar.

HAMILTON, B.

Hugh Hamilton.

Peerage, p. 40.

1661 29 Mar.

CHOLMONDELEY, V.

Robert Cholmondeley.

Remainder, failing heirs male, to brother Hugh Cholmondeley and heirs male.

Peerage, p. 25; C 231/7 p. 94; LP 13 Chas. II, pt. 3 (C 66/2958) no. 5.

1661 30 Mar.

ORMOND, D.

James Marquess of Ormond and Earl of Brecknock (E).

Peerage, p. 2; C 231/7 p. 94; LP 13 Chas. II, pt. 3 (C 66/2958) no. 4; preamble printed in Lodge, iv, 51–2.

1661 20 Apr.

TYRCONNEL, E.

Oliver Viscount Fitzwilliam.

C 231/7 p. 99; LP 13 Chas. II, pt. 2 (C 66/2957) no. 9; dated 20 Apr. 1663 (*sic*) in *Peerage*, p. 10.

1661 14 June

DROGHEDA, E.

Henry Viscount Moore.

Peerage, p. 9.

1661 18 July

MOUNT ALEXANDER, E.

Hugh Viscount Montgomery.

Peerage, p. 9.

1661 5 Sept.

FANSHAWE, V.

Sir Thomas Fanshawe, Kt.

Peerage, p. 25; C 231/7 p. 138.

1661 11 Dec.   **CASTLEMAINE, E.**; Palmer, B.
Roger Palmer.
Remainder to heirs male by wife Barbara.
Peerage, p. 9; C 231/7 p. 149; LP 13 Chas. II, pt. 23
(C 66/2978) no. 10.

1662 14 Feb.   **DUNGAN, V.**; Dungan, B.
Sir William Dungan, Bart.
Remainder, failing heirs male, to brothers and heirs
male.
Peerage, p. 25.

1662 13 May   **ARRAN, E.**; Tullogh, V.; Butler, B.
Lord Richard Butler.
Remainder, failing heirs male, to brother Lord John
Butler and heirs male.
Peerage, p. 10.

1662 26 June   **CARLINGFORD, E.**
Theobald Viscount Taaffe.
Peerage, p. 10; *LJ*, xc, 410; dated 26 June 1661 (*sic*) in
CP, iii, 28; preamble printed in Lodge, iv, 295–6.

1662 17 July   **CLARE, V.**; Moyorta, B.
Sir Daniel O'Brien, Kt.
Peerage, p. 25; dated 11 (*sic*) July 1662 in *CP*, iii, 252;
preamble printed in Lodge, ii, 32–3.

1662 28 Aug.   **DUNGANNON, V.**; Trevor, B.
Marcus Trevor.
Peerage, p. 26.

1663 14 July   **FITZHARDINGE, V.**; Berkeley, B.
Sir Charles Berkeley, Kt.
Remainder, failing heirs male, to father and heirs male.
Peerage, p. 26; C 231/7 p. 208; LP 13 Chas. II, pt. 8
(C 66/3039) no. 16.

1665 8 Oct.   **CHARLEMONT, V.**
William Baron Caulfield.
Peerage, p. 26.

1666 22 Feb.   **POWERSCOURT, V.**
Folliott Wingfield.
Peerage, p. 26; dated 22 Feb. 1665 (*sic*) in *CP*, x, 636;
preamble printed in Lodge, v, 275.

1673 23 Aug.   **BLESINGTON, V.**; Boyle, B.
Murrough Boyle.
Remainder, failing heirs male, to heirs male of father.
Peerage, p. 26; preamble printed in Lodge, i, 148.

1673 9 Oct.   **TYRONE, E.**; Decies, V.
Richard Baron Le Power and Coroghmore.
Peerage, p. 10; C 231/7 p. 463; LP 25 Chas. II, pt. 1
(C 66/3143) no. 22.

1675 21 Sept.   **DOWNE, V.**; Cloney, B.
Sir William Ducie, Bart.
C 231/7 p. 501; LP 27 Chas. II, pt. 1 (C 66/3168) no.
1; dated 19 July (*sic*) 1675 in *CP*, iv, 451.

1675 8 Nov.   **LONGFORD, V.**
Francis Baron Aungier.
Remainder, failing heirs male, to brothers and heirs
male.
Peerage, p. 26; C 231/7 p. 502; preamble printed in
Lodge, iii, 378.

1675 22 Nov.   **GRANARD, V.**; Clanehugh, B.
Sir Arthur Forbes, Bart.
Peerage, p. 26; preamble printed in Lodge, ii, 145.

1676 13 Apr.   **GOWRAN, E.**; Clonmore, V.; Butler, B.
Lord John Butler.
Peerage, p. 10.

1676 31 July   **LANESBOROUGH, V.**
Sir George Lane, Bart.
Peerage, p. 26.

1677 11 Dec.   **RANELAGH, E.**
Richard Viscount Ranelagh.
Peerage, p. 10; C 231/7 p. 537; LP 29 Chas. II, pt. 10
(C 66/3197) no. 6.

1677 18 Dec.   **LONGFORD, E.**
Francis Viscount Longford.
Remainder, failing heirs male, to brothers and heirs
male.
Peerage, p. 10; preamble printed in Lodge, iii, 378.

1681 11 Feb.   **BELLOMONT, E.**
Charles Baron Wotton (E).
Peerage, p. 10; C 231/8 p. 43; LP 33 Chas. II, pt. 1
(C 66/3219) no. 12.

1681 14 Feb.   **ALTHAM, B.**
Hon. Altham Annesley.
Remainder, failing heirs male, to younger brothers and
heirs male.
Peerage, p. 40; C 231/8 p. 47; LP 33 Chas. II, pt. 3
(C 66/3221) no. 17.

1681 19 Feb.   **DOWNE, V.**
Sir John Dawnay, Kt.
Peerage, p. 26; C 231/8 p. 43; LP 33 Chas. II, pt. 1
(C 66/3219) no. 8 printed in *LJ*, ciii, 326–7.

1681 2 July   **ROSSE, V.**; Oxmantown, B.
Sir Richard Parsons, Bart.
Peerage, p. 26.

1683 19 Mar.   **MOUNTJOY, V.**; Stewart, B.
Sir William Stewart, Bart.
Peerage, p. 26; preamble printed in Lodge, vi, 248.

1683 30 June   **WENMAN, V.**; Wenman, B.
Sir Richard Wenman, Bart.
Reversion after death of present viscount without heirs
male to self and heirs male.
C 231/8 p. 85; LP 35 Chas. II, pt. 4 (C 66/3238) no.
10; English translation printed in *Burke's Extinct Peerage*
(1883), p. 624.

1684 30 Dec.   **GRANARD, E.**
Arthur Viscount Granard.
Peerage, p. 10; preamble printed in Lodge, ii, 145.

James II

1685 20 June   **TYRCONNEL, E.**; Baltinglass, V.; Talbot, B.
Richard Talbot.
Remainder, failing heirs male, to nephews Sir William
Talbot, Bart. and William Talbot and heirs male.
Peerage, p. 10.

1686 2 Jan.   **LIMERICK, E.**
                           William Viscount Dungan.
                           Remainder, failing heirs male, to brother Thomas
                           Dungan and cousin John Dungan and heirs male.
                           Peerage, p. 10.

1686 29 Jan.   **LISBURNE, V.**; Rathfarnham, B.
                           Adam Loftus.
                           Peerage, p. 26; preamble printed in Lodge,
                           vi, 283.

1686 29 Oct.   **BELLEW, B.**
                           Sir John Bellew, Kt.
                           Peerage, p. 41.

William III and Mary II

1689 9 Apr.   **HEWETT, V.**; James Town, B.
                           Sir George Hewett, Bart.
                           Peerage, p. 26; C 231/8 p. 214; LP 1 Will. & Mary, pt. 2
                           (C 66/3326) no. 5.

1689 2 Nov.   **BELLOMONT, E.**
                           Richard Baron Coloony.
                           Peerage, p. 10; C 231/8 p. 242; LP 1 Will. & Mary, pt. 9
                           (C 66/3333) no. 7; preamble printed in Lodge, iii,
                           209–10.

1690 12 Dec.   **CUTTS, B.**
                           John Cutts.
                           Peerage, p. 41; C 231/8 p. 264; LP 2 Will. & Mary, pt. 6
                           (C 66/3339) no. 17.

1692 3 Mar.   **LEINSTER, D.**; Bangor, E.; Tara, B.
                           Meinhardt Schomberg.
                           Peerage, p. 2; dated 3 Mar. 1691 (*sic*) in *CP*, vii, 573; xi,
                           528.

1692 4 Mar.   **ATHLONE, E.**; Aghrim, B.
                           Godard van Reede.
                           Peerage, p. 10; preamble printed in Lodge, ii, 155–6.

1692 7 Apr.   **CONINGSBY, B.**
                     Thomas Coningsby.
                     Peerage, p. 41.

1692 25 Nov.   **GALWAY, V.**; Portarlington, B.
                     Henry de Massue.
                     Peerage, p. 26.

1694 8 Mar.   **ARRAN, E.**; Tullogh, V.; Butler, B.
                     Charles Baron Butler (E).
                     Peerage, p. 10; dated 8 Mar. 1693 (*sic*) in *CP*, i, 226.

William III

1695 25 June   **LISBURNE, V.**; Vaughan, B.
                     John Vaughan.
                     C 231/8 p. 340; LP 7 Will. III, pt. 1 (C 66/3378) no.
                     17; dated 5 (*sic*) June 1695 in *Peerage*, p. 26.

1697 12 May   **GALWAY, E.**
                     Henry Viscount Galway.
                     Peerage, p. 10; C 231/8 p. 368; LP 9 Will. III, pt. 1
                     (C 66/3390) no. 12.

1699 16 June   **SHELBURNE, B.**
                     Henry Petty.
                     Peerage, p. 41; dated 16 June or 26 Oct. (*sic*) 1699 in
                     CP, xi, 669; preamble printed in Lodge, ii, 359.

1699 19 July   **WINDSOR, V.**
                     Hon. Thomas Windsor Hickman.
                     Peerage, p. 26; dated 19 June (*sic*) 1699 in *CP*, xii(2),
                     804; preamble printed in Lodge, v, 84.

1701 16 May   **HOWE, V.**; Glenawly, B.
                     Sir Scrope Howe, Kt.
                     Peerage, p. 27; preamble printed in Lodge, v, 84.

1701 2 Dec.   **STRABANE, V.**; Mountcastle, B.
                     James Earl of Abercorn (S) and Baron Hamilton.
                     Peerage, p. 27; dated 2 Sept. (*sic*) 1701 in *CP*, i, 6;
                     preamble printed in Lodge, v, 122.

Anne

1703 29 Mar.   **PIERREPONT, B.**
Gervase Pierrepont.
Peerage, p. 41; C 231/9 p. 93; LP 2 Anne, pt. 2
(C 66/3439) no. 33.

1703 16 June   **FERMANAGH, V.**; Verney, B.
Sir John Verney, Bart.
C 231/9 p. 97; LP 2 Anne, pt. 3 (C 66/3440) no. 14;
dated 10 (*sic*) June 1703 in *Peerage*, p. 27.

1703 23 June   **DONERAILE, V.**; Kilmayden, B.
Arthur St. Leger.
Peerage, p. 27.

1706 21 Jan.   **MOUNTCASHELL, V.**
Paul Davis.
Peerage, p. 27.

1707 10 Jan.   **TYRAWLEY, B.**
Sir Charles O'Hara, Kt.
Peerage, p. 41; C 231/9 p. 150; LP 5 Anne, pt. 1
(C 66/3453) no. 29.

1707 15 Mar.   **CASTLECOMER, V.**; Wandesford, B.
Sir Christopher Wandesford, Bart.
Peerage, p. 27; C 231/9 p. 154; LP 6 Anne, pt. 5
(C 66/3461) no. 13.

1712 16 Oct.   **CONWAY, B.**
Francis Baron Conway (E).
Peerage, p. 41.

George I

1715 12 Apr.   **CATHERLOUGH, M.**; Rathfarnham, E.; Trim, B.
Thomas Marquess of Wharton (GB).
Peerage, p. 3.

1715 12 Apr. **NEWBOROUGH, B.**
Hon. George Cholmondeley.
Peerage, p. 41; preamble printed in Lodge, v, 68.

1715 13 Apr. **BRODRICK, B.**
Alan Brodrick.
Peerage, p. 41; preamble printed in Lodge, v, 166.

1715 16 Apr. **ST. GEORGE, B.**
Sir George St. George, Bart.
Remainder, failing heirs male, to heirs male of father.
Peerage, p. 41; dated 18 (*sic*) Apr. 1715 in *CP*, xi, 306.

1715 18 Apr. **RANELAGH, B.**
Sir Arthur Cole, Bart.
Remainder, failing heirs male, to heirs male of father.
Peerage, p. 41; preamble printed in Lodge, vi, 49.

1715 21 Apr. **PERCEVAL, B.**
Sir John Perceval, Bart.
Remainder, failing heirs male, to heirs male of father.
Peerage, p. 42; preamble printed in Lodge, ii, 260–61.

1715 27 Apr. **GOWRAN, B.**
Richard Fitzpatrick.
Peerage, p. 42; preamble printed in Lodge, ii, 347.

1715 9 May **CARBERY, B.**
George Evans.
Remainder, failing heirs male, to heirs male of father.
Peerage, p. 42; preamble printed in Lodge, vi, 41–2.

1715 9 Oct. **FERRARD, B.**
Sir Henry Tichborne, Bart.
Peerage, p. 42; dated 19 (*sic*) Oct. 1715 in *LJI*, ii, 455.

1715 20 Oct. **HAMILTON, B.**
Gustavus Hamilton.
Peerage, p. 42; preamble printed in Lodge, v, 176–7.

1715 21 Oct. **NEWTOWN BUTLER, B.**
Theophilus Butler.
Remainder, failing heirs male, to heirs male of father.
Peerage, p. 42; preamble printed in Lodge, ii, 397.

1715 22 Oct.

MOORE, B.
John Moore.
Peerage, p. 42; preamble printed in Lodge, ii, 89–90.

1716 5 July

ULSTER, E.
Prince Ernest Augustus.
Also grant of dukedom of York and Albany (GB).
C 231/9 p. 400; LP 2 Geo. I, pt. 4 (C 66/3514) no.
15; dated 29 June (*sic*) 1716 in *Peerage*, p. 10.

1716 16 July

MUNSTER, D.; Dungannon, M. & E.; Dundalk, B.
Ermengarde Melusina von der Schulenberg.
For life.
Peerage, p. 2; dated 18 (*sic*) July 1716 in *CP*, vii, 112.

1716 16 July

MOLESWORTH, V.; Molesworth, B.
Robert Molesworth.
Peerage, p. 27; preamble printed in Lodge, v, 135–6.

1716 21 July

FITZWILLIAM, E.; Milton, V.
William Baron Fitzwilliam.
Peerage, p. 11; preamble printed in Lodge, ii, 178–9.

1717 29 June

CHETWYND, V.; Rathdowne, B.
Walter Chetwynd.
Remainder, failing heirs male, to heirs male of father.
Peerage, p. 27; preamble printed in Lodge, v, 156.

1717 15 Aug.

MIDLETON, V.
Alan Baron Brodrick.
Peerage, p. 28; preamble printed in Lodge, v, 167.

1717 20 Aug.

BOYNE, V.
Gustavus Baron Hamilton.
Peerage, p. 28; LP printed in *LJ*, lxxxvii, 318–19.

1717 21 Aug.

HILLSBOROUGH, V.; Kilwarlin, B.
Trevor Hill.
Remainder, failing heirs male, to heirs male of father.
Peerage, p. 28.

1717 28 Aug.

ALLEN, V.; Allen, B.
John Allen.
Peerage, p. 28; preamble printed in Lodge, v, 184.

1717 4 Sept.	**SOUTHWELL, B**. Sir Thomas Southwell, Bart. *Peerage*, p. 42; preamble printed in Lodge, vi, 25.
1718 22 Apr.	**FANE, V.**; Loughguyre, B. Charles Fane. *Peerage*, p. 28.
1718 24 Apr.	**CASTLEMAINE, V.**; Newtown, B. Sir Richard Child, Bart. *Peerage*, p. 28.
1718 1 May	**AYLMER, B.** Matthew Aylmer. *Peerage*, p. 42; LP printed in *Claims to Vote*, ii, 81–3
1718 16 June	**ROSSE, E.** Richard Viscount Rosse. *Peerage*, p. 11.
1718 23 June	**TYRCONNEL, V.**; Charleville, B. Sir John Brownlow, Bart. *Peerage*, p. 28.
1719 29 Apr.	**SHELBURNE, E.**; Dunkeron, V. Henry Baron Shelburne. *Peerage*, p. 11; preamble printed in Lodge, ii, 359.
1719 13 May	**LIMERICK, V.**; Claneboye, B. James Hamilton. *Peerage*, p. 28; preamble printed in Lodge, iii, 11.
1719 29 May	**GRIMSTON, V.**; Dunboyne, B. Sir William Grimston, Bart. *Peerage*, p. 28; dated 28 (*sic*) May 1719 in *LJI*, ii, 612; preamble printed in Lodge, v, 197–8.
1719 29 May	**CARPENTER, B.** George Carpenter. *Peerage*, p. 42; preamble printed in Lodge, iii, 91–2.
1719 3 June	**LONDONDERRY, B.** Thomas Pitt. *Peerage*, p. 42.

1720 1 July   **BARRINGTON, V.**; Barrington, B.
                        John Shute Barrington.
                        Peerage, p. 28; preamble printed in Lodge, v, 202–03.

1720 13 Sept.   **VANE, V.**; Vane, B.
                        Hon. William Vane.
                        Peerage, p. 28.

1720 14 Sept.   **GAGE, V.**; Gage, B.
                        Sir Thomas Gage, Bart.
                        Peerage, p. 28; preamble printed in Lodge, v, 221.

1720 4 Nov.   **TYRONE, V.**; Beresford, B.
                        Sir Marcus Beresford, Bart.
                        Peerage, p. 28; preamble printed in Lodge, ii, 302–03.

1720 22 Nov.   **BLUNDELL, V.**; Blundell, B.
                        Sir Montagu Blundell, Bart.
                        Peerage, p. 28.

1721 9 Jan.   **WHITWORTH, B.**
                        Charles Whitworth.
                        Peerage, p. 42.

1721 11 Sept.   **GRANDISON, E.**
                        John Viscount Grandison.
                        Peerage, p. 11.

1721 11 Sept.   **LEINSTER, E.**
                        Sophia Charlotte von Platen.
                        For life.
                        Peerage, p. 11.

1721 11 Sept.   **BESSBOROUGH, B.**
                        William Ponsonby.
                        Peerage, p. 42; preamble printed in Lodge, ii, 274.

1721 13 Sept.   **DARCY, B.**
                        Hon. John Darcy.
                        Remainder, failing heirs male, to grandson James Darcy
                        and heirs male.
                        Peerage, p. 42.

1721 14 Sept.   **CLIFTON, B.**
                        John Bligh.
                        Peerage, p. 42.

1722 8 Feb.

KILMAINE, B.
Hon. James O'Hara.
Peerage, p. 42.

1723 17 Jan.

KERRY, E.; Clanmaurice, V.
Thomas Baron Kerry.
Peerage, p. 11; LP printed in *Claims to Vote*, iii,
251–2.

1723 25 Feb.

PERCEVAL, V.
John Baron Perceval.
Peerage, p. 28.

1723 28 Feb.

DUNCANNON, V.
William Baron Bessborough.
Peerage, p. 29.

1723 7 Mar.

DARNLEY, V.
John Baron Clifton.
Peerage, p. 29.

1723 12 Mar.

PALMERSTON, V.; Temple, B.
Henry Temple.
Remainder, failing heirs male, to brother John Temple
and heirs male.
Peerage, p. 29; preamble printed in Lodge, v, 243.

1724 14 Aug.

MICKLETHWAITE, B.
Joseph Micklethwaite.
Peerage, p. 42.

1725 29 June

DARNLEY, E.
John Viscount Darnley.
Peerage, p. 11; LP printed in *Claims to Vote*, ii,
251–2.

1725 12 July

BATEMAN, V.; Culmore, B.
William Bateman.
Peerage, p. 29.

1726 8 Oct.

LONDONDERRY, E.; Gallen-Ridgeway, V.
Thomas Baron Londonderry.
Peerage, p. 11.

Creations 1603–1898

George II

1727 6 June	**MICKLETHWAITE, V.** Joseph Baron Micklethwaite. *Peerage*, p. 29.

1727 6 June   **MICKLETHWAITE, V.**
Joseph Baron Micklethwaite.
Peerage, p. 29.

1727 17 July   **GALWAY, V.**; Killard, B.
John Monckton.
Peerage, p. 29.

1728 12 Aug.   **LANESBOROUGH, V.**
Brinsley Baron Newtown Butler.
Peerage, p. 29.

1731 11 June   **TYLNEY, E.**
Richard Viscount Castlemaine.
Peerage, p. 11 where '11 Jan.' is evidently a misprint for '11 June'; *CP*, iii, 92.

1731 17 Sept.   **WYNDHAM, B.**
Thomas Wyndham.
Peerage, p. 43.

1733 4 Oct.   **CATHERLOUGH, B**.
Hon. John Fane.
Peerage, p. 43

1733 27 Oct.   **CASTLE DURROW, B.**
William Flower.
Peerage, p. 43; preamble printed in Lodge, v, 286–7.

1733 6 Nov.   **EGMONT, E.**
John Viscount Perceval.
Peerage, p. 11; preamble printed in Lodge, ii, 262–3.

1733 10 Nov.   **DESART, B.**
John Cuffe.
Peerage, p. 43; preamble printed in Lodge, vi, 62–3.

1735 2 June   **SUNDON, B.**
William Clayton.
Peerage, p. 43.

1735 28 July

BRACO, B.
William Duff.
Peerage, p. 43.

1738 16 Mar.

BELFIELD, B.
Robert Rochfort.
Peerage, p. 43.

1739 6 Oct.

BESSBOROUGH, E.
Brabazon Viscount Duncannon.
Peerage, p. 12; preamble printed in Lodge, ii, 278.

1743 22 Mar.

VERNEY, E.
Ralph Viscount Fermanagh.
Peerage, p. 12.

1743 2 May

PANMURE, E.; Maule, V.
William Maule.
Remainder, failing heirs male, to brother John Maule
and heirs male.
Peerage, p. 12; dated 6 Apr. (*sic*) 1743 in *CP*, x, 306.

1743 29 Nov.

NEWPORT, B.
Robert Jocelyn.
Peerage, p. 43.

1744 4 Feb.

POWERSCOURT, V.; Wingfield, B.
Richard Wingfield.
Peerage, p. 29; preamble printed in Lodge, v, 277–8.

1745 7 Dec.

BLESINGTON, E.
William Viscount Mountjoy.
Peerage, p. 12.

1746 10 Apr.

GRANDISON, V.
Lady Elizabeth Mason.
Peerage, p. 29.

1746 9 July

MORNINGTON, B.
Richard Wesley.
Peerage, p. 43.

1746 18 July

TYRONE, E.
Marcus Viscount Tyrone.
Peerage, p. 12; preamble printed in Lodge, ii, 303.

1746 8 Aug. **LUXBOROUGH, B.**
Robert Knight.
Peerage, p. 43; dated 8 Aug. 1745 (*sic*) in *CP*, iii, 110.

1746 15 Aug. **FORTESCUE, B.**
Sir John Fortescue Aland, Kt.
Peerage, p. 43.

1748 10 June **CARRICK, E.**
Somerset Hamilton Viscount Ikerrin.
Peerage, p. 12.

1748 13 June **KINGSBOROUGH, B.**
Sir Robert King, Bart.
Peerage, p. 43; preamble printed in Lodge, iii, 236.

1750 9 Apr. **RAWDON, B.**
Sir John Rawdon, Bart.
Peerage, p. 43.

1750 10 Apr. **KNAPTON, B.**
Sir John Denny Vesey, Bart.
Peerage, p. 43.

1750 17 Dec. **MALTON, E.**; Malton, B.
Charles Marquess of Rockingham (GB).
Peerage, p. 12; dated 17 Sept. (*sic*) 1750 in *CP*, xi, 60.

1751 30 Sept. **ASHBROOK, V.**
Henry Baron Castle Durrow.
Peerage, p. 29.

1751 3 Oct. **HILLSBOROUGH, E.**; Kilwarlin, V.
Wills Viscount Hillsborough.
Remainder, failing heirs male, to uncle Arthur Hill and heirs male.
Peerage, p. 12.

1751 5 Oct. **UPPER OSSORY, E.**
John Baron Gowran.
Peerage, p. 13.

1751 5 Oct. **BELFIELD, V.**
Robert Baron Belfield.
Peerage, p. 29.

1751 5 Oct.	**LOFTUS, B.** Nicholas Loftus. *Peerage*, p. 43; preamble printed in Lodge, vi, 266–7.
1751 7 Oct.	**FITZMAURICE, V.**; Dunkeron, B. Hon. John Petty. *Peerage*, p. 29.
1752 23 Jan.	**CARYSFORT, B.** John Proby. *Peerage*, p. 43.
1753 26 June	**SHELBURNE, E.** John Viscount Fitzmaurice. *Peerage*, p. 13; LP printed in *Claims to Vote*, iii, 283–4; dated 6 (*sic*) June 1753 in *Peerage*, p. 54 and *CP*, xi, 650.
1753 3 July	**MILTON, B.** Joseph Damer. *Peerage*, p. 43.
1753 3 Oct.	**CONYNGHAM, B.** Henry Conyngham. *Peerage*, p. 43.
1753 8 Nov.	**POLLINGTON, B.** Sir John Savile, Kt. *Peerage*, p. 43.
1755 6 Dec.	**JOCELYN, V.** Robert Baron Newport. *Peerage*, p. 29.
1755 19 Dec.	**LUDLOW, B.** Peter Ludlow. *Peerage*, p. 43.
1756 17 Apr.	**SHANNON, E.**; Boyle, V.; Castle Martyr, B. Henry Boyle. *Peerage*, p. 14; dated 7 (*sic*) Apr. 1756 in *ibid*. p. 53 and *CP*, xi, 657.
1756 4 May	**MOUNTMORRES, B.** Hervey Morres. *Peerage*, p. 43.

1756 5 May   **RUSSBOROUGH, B.**
Joseph Leeson.
Peerage, p. 43.

1756 6 May   **FARNHAM, B.**
John Maxwell.
Peerage, p. 43.

1756 7 May   **LONGFORD, B.**
Thomas Pakenham.
Peerage, p. 43.

1756 16 July   **MASSEREENE, E.**
Clotworthy Viscount Massereene.
Peerage, p. 14; dated 28 (*sic*) July 1756 in *CP*, viii, 546.

1756 19 July   **LOFTUS, V.**
Nicholas Baron Loftus.
Peerage, p. 30.

1756 20 July   **LANESBOROUGH, E.**
Humphrey Viscount Lanesborough.
Peerage, p. 14.

1756 20 July   **CONYNGHAM, V.**
Henry Baron Conyngham.
Peerage, p. 30.

1756 24 Nov.   **CLANBRASSIL, E.**
James Viscount Limerick.
Peerage, p. 14.

1756 29 Nov.   **BELVIDERE, E.**
Robert Viscount Belfield.
Peerage, p. 14.

1756 11 Dec.   **THOMOND, E.;** Ibrackan, B.
Percy Wyndham O'Brien.
Peerage, p. 14.

1756 18 Dec.   **BLAKENEY, B.**
Sir William Blakeney, Kt.
Peerage, p. 43.

1757 21 Dec.   **LIGONIER, V.**
Sir John Louis Ligonier, Kt.
Peerage, p. 30; dated 31 (*sic*) Dec. 1757 in *CP*, vii, 655.

1758 15 Aug.   **WANDESFORD, E.**
John Viscount Castlecomer.
Peerage, p. 14.

1758 15 Aug.   **SUDLEY, V.**; Saunders, B.
Sir Arthur Gore, Bart.
Peerage, p. 30.

1758 15 Aug.   **BOWES, B.**
John Bowes.
Peerage, p. 44.

1758 15 Sept.   **BRANDON, E.**
Ellis Dowager Lady Athenry.
For life.
Peerage, p. 14.

1758 16 Sept.   **CHARLEVILLE, E.**
Charles Baron Moore.
Peerage, p. 14.

1758 16 Sept.   **BRANDEN, B.**
Sir Maurice Crosbie, Kt.
Peerage, p. 44.

1758 18 Sept.   **LISLE, B.**
John Lysaght.
Peerage, p. 44.

1758 19 Sept.   **COURTOWN, B.**
James Stopford.
Peerage, p. 44.

1758 20 Sept.   **ANNESLEY, B.**
William Annesley.
Peerage, p. 44; LP printed in *LJ*, lxxxvii, 366–7.

1759 23 Apr.   **LOUTH, E.**
Thomas Baron Athenry.
Peerage, p. 14.

1759 26 Apr. **FIFE, E.**; Macduff, V.
William Baron Braco.
Peerage, p. 14.

1760 1 Apr. **ULSTER, E.**
Prince Edward Augustus.
Also grant of dukedom of York and Albany
(GB).
C 231/11 p. 258; LP 33 Geo. III, pt. 4 (C 66/3668)
no. 20.

1760 6 Sept. **HEADFORT, B.**
Sir Thomas Taylour, Bart.
Peerage, p. 44.

1760 8 Sept. **RUSSBOROUGH, V.**
Joseph Baron Russborough.
Peerage, p. 30.

1760 8 Sept. **MOUNTFLORENCE, B.**
John Cole.
Peerage, p. 44.

1760 10 Sept. **FARNHAM, V.**
Robert Baron Farnham.
Peerage, p. 30.

1760 10 Sept. **MONTEAGLE, B.**
John Browne.
Peerage, p. 44.

1760 11 Sept. **HOLMES, B.**
Thomas Holmes.
Peerage, p. 44.

1760 2 Oct. **MORNINGTON, E.**; Wellesley, V.
Garret Baron Mornington.
Peerage, p. 14.

1760 3 Oct. **LUDLOW, E.**; Preston, V.
Peter Baron Ludlow.
Peerage, p. 15.

George III

1761 19 Mar.   **KILDARE, M.**; Offaly, E.
James Earl of Kildare and Viscount Leinster
(GB).
Peerage, p. 3; dated 3 (*sic*) Mar. 1761 in *CP*, vii, 245,
574.

1761 10 Apr.   **WINTERTON, B.**
Edward Turnour.
Peerage, p. 44; LP printed in *Claims to Vote*, iv,
Winterton petition, pp. 4–5.

1761 1 May   **TYRCONNEL, E.**; Carlingford, V.
George Baron Carpenter.
Peerage, p. 15.

1762 30 Jan.   **MOIRA, E.**
John Baron Rawdon.
Peerage, p. 15.

1762 26 Feb.   **COLERAINE, B**.
Gabriel Hanger.
Peerage, p. 44.

1762 15 Mar.   **CLIVE, B.**
Robert Clive.
Peerage, p. 44; LP printed in *LJ*, xciii, 567.

1762 7 Apr.   **ORWELL, B.**
Francis Vernon.
Peerage, p. 44.

1762 12 Apr.   **ARRAN, E.**
Arthur Viscount Sudley.
Peerage, p. 16.

1762 12 Apr.   **COURTOWN, E.**; Stopford, V.
James Baron Courtown.
Peerage, p. 16.

1762 12 Apr.   **HEADFORT, V.**
Thomas Baron Headfort.
Peerage, p. 30.

1762 20 May
LIGONIER, V.
John Louis Viscount Ligonier.
Remainder, failing heirs male, to Edward Ligonier and
heirs male.
Peerage, p. 30.

1762 22 June
WALTHAM, B.
John Olmius.
Peerage, p. 44.

1763 10 May
MILLTOWN, E.
Joseph Viscount Russborough.
Peerage, p. 16.

1763 13 May
FARNHAM, E.
Robert Viscount Farnham.
Peerage, p. 16.

1763 14 May
CATHERLOUGH, E.; Barrells, V.
Robert Baron Luxborough.
Peerage, p. 16.

1763 21 May
BALTINGLASS, B.
John Stratford.
Peerage, p. 44.

1763 24 May
ST. GEORGE, B.
Usher St. George.
Peerage, p. 44; dated 19 Apr. (*sic*) 1763 in *CP*, xi, 307.

1763 29 June
MOUNTMORRES, V.
Hervey Baron Mountmorres.
Peerage, p. 30.

1763 23 Dec.
CHARLEMONT, E.
James Viscount Charlemont.
Peerage, p. 16.

1764 30 June
GORE, B.
Sir Ralph Gore, Bart.
Peerage, p. 44.

1764 13 July
KINGSTON, B.
Sir Edward King, Bart.
Peerage, p. 44; preamble printed in Lodge, iii, 237.

1764 14 July

KILWORTH, B.
Stephen Moore.
Peerage, pp. 18, 56; dated 13 (*sic*) July 1764 in *ibid*.
p. 44 and *CP*, ix, 311.

1764 19 Nov.

CONNAUGHT, E.
Prince William Henry.
Also grant of dukedom of Gloucester and Edinburgh
(GB).
C 231/12 p. 21; LP 5 Geo. III, pt. 1 (C 66/3698)
no. 21.

1766 17 Jan.

ANNALY, B.
John Gore.
Peerage, p. 44.

1766 18 Jan.

PIGOT, B.
Sir George Pigot, Bart.
Peerage, p. 44.

1766 22 Jan.

MOUNTCASHELL, V.
Stephen Baron Kilworth.
Peerage, p. 30.

1766 11 Feb.

MEXBOROUGH, E.; Pollington, V.
John Baron Pollington.
Peerage, p. 16.

1766 12 Feb.

WINTERTON, E.; Turnour, V.
Edward Baron Winterton.
Peerage, p. 16; LP printed in *LJ*, civ, 416–17.

1766 17 Feb.

DUNGANNON, V.; Hill, B.
Arthur Trevor.
Peerage, p. 30.

1766 19 Feb.

LANGFORD, V.; Somerhill, B.
Elizabeth Ormsby Rowley.
Remainder to heirs male by husband.
Peerage, p. 30.

1766 22 Oct.

DUBLIN, E.
Prince Henry Frederick.
Also grant of dukedom of Gloucester and Strathearn
(GB).
C 231/12 p. 57; LP 6 Geo. III, pt. 6 (C 66/3709)
no. 3.

1766 23 Oct.   **ELY, E.**
Nicholas Viscount Loftus.
Peerage, p. 16.

1766 24 Oct.   **BECTIVE, E.**
Thomas Viscount Headfort.
Peerage, p. 16.

1766 14 Nov.   **GLERAWLEY, V.**
William Baron Annesley.
Peerage, p. 30; LP printed in *LJ*, lxxxvii, 367.

1766 15 Nov.   **KINGSTON, V.**
Edward Baron Kingston.
Peerage, p. 30.

1766 17 Nov.   **CLANWILLIAM, V.**; Gillford, B.
Sir John Meade, Bart.
Peerage, p. 30.

1766 18 Nov.   **FORTROSE, V.**; Ardelve, B.
Kenneth Mackenzie.
Peerage, p. 30.

1766 26 Nov.   **LEINSTER, D.**
James Marquess of Kildare and Viscount Leinster (GB).
Peerage, p. 2.

1767 19 Jan.   **CLARE, V.**; Nugent, B.
Robert Nugent.
Peerage, p. 30.

1767 19 Feb.   **GRANDISON, E.**; Villiers, V.
Elizabeth Viscountess Grandison.
Peerage, p. 16.

1767 3 Sept.   **HOWTH, E.**; St. Lawrence, V.
Thomas Baron Howth.
Peerage, p. 16.

1767 3 Sept.   **MULGRAVE, B.**
Constantine Phipps.
Peerage, p. 44.

1767 4 Sept.   **BELLOMONT, E.**
                     Charles Baron Coloony.
                     Peerage, p. 16.

1768 9 Jan.   **LIFFORD, B.**
                     James Hewitt.
                     Peerage, p. 44.

1768 14 July   **SYDNEY, B.**
                     Dudley Alexander Sydney Cosby.
                     Peerage, p. 44.

1768 15 July   **ERNE, B.**
                     Abraham Creighton.
                     Peerage, p. 44.

1768 16 July   **EYRE, B.**
                     John Eyre.
                     Peerage, p. 45.

1768 24 Aug.   **WESTPORT, V.**
                     John Baron Monteagle.
                     Peerage, p. 30.

1768 25 Aug.   **KINGSTON, E.**
                     Edward Viscount Kingston.
                     Peerage, p. 17.

1768 25 Aug.   **BELLISLE, V.**
                     Ralph Baron Gore.
                     Peerage, p. 31.

1768 13 Oct.   **IRNHAM, B.**
                     Simon Luttrell.
                     Peerage, p. 45.

1770 23 May   **ARDEN, B.**
                     Catharine Countess of Egmont.
                     Peerage, p. 45.

1770 26 May   **CLERMONT, B.**
                     William Henry Fortescue.
                     Peerage, p. 45.

1770 28 May   **DARTREY, B.**
                         Thomas Dawson.
                         Peerage, p. 45.

1770 29 May   **DAWSON, B.**
                         William Henry Dawson.
                         Peerage, p. 45.

1770 30 May   **BANGOR, B.**
                         Bernard Ward.
                         Peerage, p. 45.

1770 28 June   **MELBOURNE, B.**
                         Sir Peniston Lamb, Bart.
                         Peerage, p. 45; dated 8 (*sic*) June 1770 in *ibid.* p. 31 and
                         CP, viii, 635.

1771 30 Nov.   **SEFTON, E.**
                         Charles William Viscount Molyneux.
                         Peerage, p. 17.

1771 30 Nov.   **CROSBIE, V.**
                         William Baron Branden.
                         Peerage, p. 31.

1771 1 Dec.   **RODEN, E.**
                         Robert Viscount Jocelyn.
                         Peerage, p. 17.

1771 2 Dec.   **ELY, E.**
                         Henry Viscount Loftus.
                         Peerage, p. 17.

1771 3 Dec.   **SEAFORTH, E.**
                         Kenneth Viscount Fortrose.
                         Peerage, p. 17.

1771 4 Dec.   **ALTAMONT, E.**
                         John Viscount Westport.
                         Peerage, p. 17.

1772 4 Jan.   **ROSS, E.**
                         Ralph Viscount Bellisle.
                         Peerage, p. 17.

1776 18 July   **LISBURNE, E.**
Wilmot Viscount Lisburne.
LJ, liv, 541; *CP*, viii, 36; dated 16 (*sic*) July 1776 in
Peerage, p. 17.

1776 18 July   **SOUTHWELL, V.**
Thomas George Baron Southwell.
Peerage, p. 31.

1776 18 July   **DE MONTALT, B.**
Sir Thomas Maude, Bart.
CP, iv, 176.

1776 19 July   **LIGONIER, E.**
Edward Viscount Ligonier.
CP, vii, 656.

1776 19 July   **DE VESCI, V.**
Thomas Baron Knapton.
Peerage, p. 31; LP printed in *LJ*, lxxxviii, 88.

1776 19 July   **MACARTNEY, B.**
Sir George Macartney, Kt.
Peerage, p. 45.

1776 20 July   **CLANWILLIAM, E.**
John Viscount Clanwilliam.
Peerage, p. 17.

1776 20 July   **ENNISKILLEN, V.**
William Willoughby Baron Mountflorence.
Peerage, p. 59; *CP*, v, 82; dated 24 June (*sic*) in *Peerage*,
p. 31.

1776 20 July   **GOSFORD, B.**
Sir Archibald Acheson, Bart.
Peerage, p. 58.

1776 21 July   **NUGENT, E.**
Robert Viscount Clare.
Remainder, failing heirs male, to son in law George
Grenville and heirs male.
Peerage, p. 17.

1776 21 July   **ORWELL, V.**
                      Francis Baron Orwell.
                      CP, xi, 681.

1776 21 July   **CLONMORE, B.**
                      Ralph Howard.
                      Peerage, p. 31; *CP*, iii, 333; dated 24 (*sic*) July 1776 in
                      Peerage, p. 58.

1776 22 July   **GLANDORE, E.**
                      William Viscount Crosbie.
                      Peerage, p. 17.

1776 22 July   **ALDBOROUGH, V.**
                      John Baron Baltinglass.
                      Peerage, p. 18.

1776 22 July   **MILFORD, B.**
                      Sir Richard Philipps, Bart.
                      Peerage, p. 45.

1776 23 July   **CLERMONT, V.**; Clermont, B.
                      William Henry Baron Clermont.
                      Remainder, failing heirs male, to brother James
                      Fortescue and heirs male.
                      Peerage, p. 18.

1776 23 July   **NEWBOROUGH, B.**
                      Sir Thomas Wynn, Bart.
                      CP, ix, 508; dated 14 (*sic*) July 1776 in *Peerage*, p. 45.

1776 24 July   **CARLOW, V.**
                      William Henry Baron Dawson.
                      Peerage, p. 59.

1776 24 July   **LUCAN, B.**
                      Sir Charles Bingham, Bart.
                      Peerage, p. 45.

1776 25 July   **MACDONALD, B.**
                      Sir Alexander Macdonald, Bart.
                      LJ, lxiii, 279; *CP*, viii, 339 ; dated 17 (*sic*) July 1776 in
                      Peerage, p. 45.

1776 26 July

NEWHAVEN, B.
Sir William Mayne, Bart.
Peerage, p. 60; *CP*, ix, 541; dated 18 (*sic*) July 1776 in
Peerage, p. 45.

1776 27 July

CLIFDEN, B.
James Agar.
Peerage, p. 58.

1776 28 July

KENSINGTON, B.
William Edwardes.
LP printed in *LJ*, lxxxv, 110–11; dated 22 (*sic*) July
1776 in *Peerage*, p. 45.

1776 29 July

WESTCOTE, B.
William Henry Lyttelton.
CP, viii, 312; dated 29 Apr. (*sic*) 1776 in *Peerage*, p. 45.

1776 30 July

ONGLEY, B.
Robert Henley Ongley.
Peerage, p. 45.

1776 31 July

SHULDHAM, B.
Molyneux Shuldham.
Peerage, p. 45.

1776 1 Aug.

NAAS, B.
John Bourke.
Peerage, p. 58.

1776 2 Aug.

DONERAILE, B.
St. Leger St. Leger.
Peerage, p. 59.

1776 3 Aug.

TEMPLETOWN, B.
Clotworthy Upton.
Peerage, p. 46.

1776 4 Aug.

MASSY, B.
Hugh Massy.
Peerage, p. 46; LP printed in *LJ*, lxxxviii, 384.

1777 8 Feb.

SHIPBROOK, E.
Francis Viscount Orwell.
CP, xi, 681.

1777 9 Feb.   **ALDBOROUGH, E.**; Amiens, V.
                    John Viscount Aldborough.
                    Peerage, p. 18.

1777 10 Feb.   **CLERMONT, E.**
                    William Henry Viscount Clermont.
                    Peerage, p. 18.

1777 26 Feb.   **ROKEBY, B.**
                    Richard Robinson, Archbishop of Armagh.
                    Remainder, failing heirs male, to brothers and heirs
                    male, failing whom to cousin Matthew Robinson and
                    heirs male.
                    Peerage, p. 46.

1781 4 Jan.   **CONYNGHAM, E.**; Conyngham, B.
                    Henry Viscount Conyngham.
                    Remainder, failing heirs male, to nephew Francis
                    Pierpont Burton and heirs male.
                    Peerage, p. 60.

1781 4 Jan.   **LIFFORD, V.**
                    James Baron Lifford.
                    Peerage, p. 31; LP printed in *LJ*, lxxxvii, 319–20; dated
                    8 (*sic*) Jan. 1781 in *CP*, vii, 652.

1781 4 Jan.   **TRACTON, B.**
                    James Dennis.
                    Peerage, p. 60.

1781 5 Jan.   **MOUNTCASHELL, E.**
                    Stephen Viscount Mountcashell.
                    Peerage, p. 18.

1781 5 Jan.   **DESART, V.**
                    Otway Baron Desart.
                    Peerage, p. 60; dated 6 (*sic*) Jan. 1781 in *ibid*. p. 31 and
                    CP, iv, 228.

1781 5 Jan.   **MUSKERRY, B.**
                    Sir Robert Tilson Deane, Bart.
                    Peerage, p. 46.

1781 6 Jan.   **ERNE, V.**
                    John Baron Erne.
                    Peerage, p. 31.

1781 6 Jan.   **BELMORE, B.**
Armar Lowry Corry.
Peerage, p. 46.

1781 8 Jan.   **FARNHAM, V.**
Barry Baron Farnham.
Peerage, p. 60; dated 10 (*sic*) Jan. 1781 in *CP*, v, 259.

1781 8 Jan.   **WELLES, B.**
Thomas Knox.
Peerage, p. 46.

1781 9 Jan.   **CARHAMPTON, V.**
Simon Baron Irnham.
Peerage, p. 60.

1781 9 Jan.   **SHEFFIELD, B.**
John Baker Holroyd.
Peerage, p. 66.

1781 10 Jan.   **BANGOR, V.**
Bernard Baron Bangor.
LJ, lxi, 459; dated 11 (*sic*) Jan. 1781 in *CP*, i, 413 and
13 (*sic*) Jan. 1781 in *Peerage*, p. 31.

1781 11 Jan.   **MELBOURNE, V.**
Peniston Baron Melbourne.
Peerage, p. 31.

1781 12 Jan.   **CLIFDEN, V.**
James Baron Clifden.
Peerage, p. 31.

1781 13 Jan.   **MAYO, V.**
John Baron Naas.
Peerage, p. 60; dated 3 (*sic*) Jan. 1781 in *ibid*. p. 18.

1782 12 Sept.   **HOOD, B.**
Sir Samuel Hood, Bart.
Peerage, p. 46.

1783 20 Sept.   **SHEFFIELD, B.**
John Baker Baron Sheffield.
Remainder, failing heirs male, to two daughters and
heirs male.
Peerage, p. 46; *CP*, vi, 664.

1783 10 Oct.   **HARBERTON, B.**
                            Arthur Pomeroy.
                            Peerage, p. 46.

1783 11 Oct.   **LEITRIM, B.**
                            Robert Clements.
                            Peerage, p. 46.

1783 12 Oct.   **LANDAFF, B.**
                            Francis Mathew.
                            Peerage, p. 46.

1783 13 Oct.   **RIVERSDALE, B.**
                            William Tonson.
                            Peerage, p. 46.

1783 16 Oct.   **DONOUGHMORE, B.**
                            Christiana Hely Hutchinson.
                            Peerage, p. 46; *CP*, iv, 400.

1783 17 Oct.   **DELAVAL, B.**
                            Sir John Hussey Delaval, Bart.
                            CP, iv, 138; dated 7 (*sic*) Oct. 1783 in *Peerage*, p. 46.

1783 21 Oct.   **MUNCASTER, B.**
                            John Pennington.
                            Remainder, failing heirs male, to brother Lowther
                            Pennington and heirs male.
                            Peerage, p. 46.

1783 19 Nov.   **PENRHYN, B.**
                            Richard Pennant.
                            Peerage, p. 47.

1784 10 May   **EARLSFORT, B.**
                            John Scott.
                            Peerage, p. 47; dated 20 (*sic*) May 1784 in *CP*, iii,
                            331.

1784 29 Nov.   **ULSTER, E.**
                            Prince Frederick.
                            Also grant of dukedom of York and Albany (GB).
                            C 231/12 p. 371; LP 25 Geo. III, pt. 1 (C 66/3816)
                            no. 3.

1785 19 June   **ANTRIM, E.**; Dunluce, V.
Randal William Earl of Antrim.
Remainder, failing heirs male, to daughters and heirs male.
LP printed in *LJ*, xc, 409–10.

1785 19 June   **CREMORNE, V.**
Thomas Baron Dartrey.
Peerage, p. 32.

1785 20 June   **LONGFORD, E.**
Elizabeth Dowager Baroness Longford.
Peerage, p. 18.

1785 20 June   **GOSFORD, V.**
Archibald Baron Gosford.
Peerage, p. 32.

1785 21 June   **PORTARLINGTON, E.**
John Viscount Carlow.
Peerage, p. 18.

1785 21 June   **WICKLOW, V.**
Ralph Baron Clonmore.
Peerage, p. 63; *LJ*, ci, 245; dated 12 (*sic*) June 1785 in *Peerage*, p. 31.

1785 22 June   **FARNHAM, E.**
Barry Viscount Farnham.
Peerage, p. 18.

1785 22 June   **DONERAILE, V.**
St. Leger Baron Doneraile.
Peerage, p. 31; LP printed in *LJ*, lxxxvi, 231–2.

1785 23 June   **CARHAMPTON, E.**
Simon Viscount Carhampton.
Peerage, p. 18.

1785 24 June   **MAYO, E.**
John Viscount Mayo.
Peerage, p. 18.

1785 27 June   **LISMORE, B.**
Cornelius O'Callaghan.
Peerage, p. 47.

1785 28 June   **LOFTUS, B.**
                        Charles Tottenham Loftus.
                        Peerage, p. 47.

1785 29 June   **DE MONTALT, B.**
                        Sir Cornwallis Maude, Bart.
                        Peerage, p. 47.

1785 30 June   **SUNDERLIN, B.**
                        Richard Malone.
                        Peerage, p. 47.

1785 30 Dec.   **PERY, V.**
                        Edmond Sexten Pery.
                        Peerage, p. 62; *CP*, x, 495; dated 30 Mar. (*sic*) 1785 in
                        Peerage, p. 31.

1789 20 May   **MUNSTER, E.**
                        Prince William Henry.
                        Also grant of dukedom of Clarence and St. Andrews
                        (GB).
                        C 231/13 p. 30; LP 29 Geo. III, pt. 2 (C 66/3847)
                        no. 1.

1789 6 July   **FITZGIBBON, B.**
                        John Fitzgibbon.
                        Peerage, p. 62.

1789 17 Aug.   **CLANRICARDE, M.**
                        Henry Earl of Clanricarde.
                        Peerage, p. 65.

1789 17 Aug.   **ANNESLEY, E.**
                        Francis Charles Viscount Glerawly.
                        Remainder, failing heirs male, to brother Hon. Richard
                        Annesley and heirs male.
                        Peerage, p. 63; LP printed in *LJ*, lxxxvii, 367–8.

1789 17 Aug.   **CLONMELL, V.**
                        John Baron Earlsfort.
                        Peerage, p. 62; dated 18 (*sic*) Aug. 1789 in *CP*, iii, 331.

1789 18 Aug.   **ANTRIM, M.**
                        Randal William Earl of Antrim.
                        Peerage, p. 62; LP printed in *Claims to Vote*, ii, 40–41.

1789 18 Aug.	**ENNISKILLEN, E.** William Willoughby Viscount Enniskillen. *Peerage*, p. 63.
1789 19 Aug.	**WATERFORD, M.** George de la Poer Earl of Tyrone and Baron Tyrone (GB). *Peerage*, p. 62.
1789 19 Aug.	**ERNE, E.** John Viscount Erne. *Peerage*, p. 63.
1789 20 Aug.	**DOWNSHIRE, M.** Wills Earl of Hillsborough and Earl of Hillsborough (GB). *Peerage*, p. 62.
1789 20 Aug.	**CARYSFORT, E.** John Joshua Baron Carysfort. *Peerage*, p. 62.
1789 17 Sept.	**CARLETON, B.** Hugh Carleton. *Peerage*, p. 63.
1789 18 Sept.	**AUCKLAND, B.** William Eden. *Dictionary of National Biography*; dated 18 Nov. (*sic*) 1789 in *CP*, i, 334.
1789 19 Sept.	**MOUNTJOY, B.** Luke Gardiner. *Peerage*, p, 63.
1789 20 Sept.	**LONDONDERRY, B.** Robert Stewart. *Peerage*, p. 63.
1789 21 Sept.	**KILMAINE, B.** Sir John Browne, Bart. *Peerage*, p. 63.
1789 22 Sept.	**CLONCURRY, B.** Sir Nicholas Lawless, Bart. *Peerage*, p. 63; LP printed in *LJ*, lxxxvi, 230; dated 29 (*sic*) Sept. 1789 in *CP*, iii, 329.

1789 23 Sept.   **ANNALY, B.**
                             Henry Gore.
                             Peerage, p. 63.

1789 24 Sept.   **EARDLEY, B.**
                             Sir Sampson Eardley, Bart.
                             CP, v, 1.

1789 26 Dec.   **BELMORE, V.**
                             Armar Lowry Baron Belmore.
                             Peerage, p. 63; dated 6 (*sic*) Dec. 1789 in *CP*, ii,
                             110–11.

1789 27 Dec.   **CONYNGHAM, V.**
                             Henry Baron Conyngham.
                             Peerage, p. 62; dated 6 (*sic*) Dec. 1789 in *CP*, iii, 411.

1789 28 Dec.   **LOFTUS, V.**
                             Charles Baron Loftus.
                             Peerage, p. 63.

1790 2 June   **GLENTWORTH, B.**
                             William Cecil Pery, Bishop of Limerick.
                             Peerage, p. 64.

1790 4 June   **CALLAN, B.**
                             George Agar.
                             Peerage, p. 64.

1790 5 June   **CLONBROCK, B.**
                             Robert Dillon.
                             Peerage, p. 63.

1790 5 June   **ORIEL, B.**
                             Margaretta Amelia Foster.
                             CP, x, 92.

1790 6 June   **CALEDON, B.**
                             James Alexander.
                             Peerage, p. 63.

1791 26 Jan.   **ST. HELENS, B.**
                             Alleyne Fitzherbert.
                             CP, xi, 315.

1791 4 July   **DONEGALL, M.**; Belfast, E.
Arthur Earl of Donegall and Baron Fisherwick (GB).
LJ, liv, 562.

1791 4 July   **NORTHLAND, V.**
Thomas Baron Welles.
Peerage, p. 64; dated 5 (*sic*) July 1791 in *CP*, ix, 701.

1791 5 July   **DROGHEDA, M.**
Charles Earl of Drogheda.
Peerage, p. 66.

1791 5 July   **HARBERTON, V.**
Arthur Baron Harberton.
Peerage, p. 64.

1792 13 June   **FERMANAGH, B.**
Mary Verney.
CP, v, 296.

1792 15 June   **WATERPARK, B.**
Sarah Lady Cavendish.
CP, xii(2), 426.

1792 19 July   **MACARTNEY, V.**
George Baron Macartney.
CP, viii, 324.

1792 22 Sept.   **OXMANTOWN, B.**
Laurence Harman Harman.
Remainder, failing heirs male, to nephew Sir Laurence
Parsons, Bart. and heirs male.
Peerage, p. 64; dated 25 (*sic*) Sept. 1792 in *CP*, xi, 168.

1793 25 Oct.   **O'NEILL, B.**
John O'Neill.
Peerage, p. 65.

1793 26 Nov.   **BANDON, B.**
Francis Bernard.
Peerage, p. 65.

1793 2 Dec.   **KILKENNY, E.**
Edmund Viscount Mountgarret.
Peerage, p. 65; LP printed in *Claims to Vote*, iii, 408–09.

1793 2 Dec.   **CASTLE STEWART, V.**
                             Andrew Thomas Stewart.
                             Peerage, p. 65; dated 20 (*sic*) Dec. 1793 in *CP*, iii, 98.

1793 3 Dec.   **MOUNTNORRIS, E.**
                             Arthur Viscount Valentia.
                             Peerage, p. 65.

1793 3 Dec.   **LEITRIM, V.**
                             Robert Baron Leitrim.
                             Peerage, p. 65; dated 20 (*sic*) Dec. 1793 in *CP*, vii,
                             580.

1793 4 Dec.   **DESART, E.**; Castle-Cuffe, V.
                             Otway Viscount Desart.
                             Peerage, p. 65.

1793 4 Dec.   **LANDAFF, V.**
                             Francis Baron Landaff.
                             Peerage, p. 65.

1793 5 Dec.   **WICKLOW, E.**
                             Alice Dowager Viscountess Wicklow.
                             LP printed in *LJ*, cii, 152–3.

1793 5 Dec.   **HAWARDEN, V.**
                             Cornwallis Baron de Montalt.
                             Peerage, p. 65; LP printed in *Claims to Vote*, ii, 465–6.

1793 6 Dec.   **CLONMELL, E.**
                             John Viscount Clonmell.
                             Peerage, p. 65.

1793 6 Dec.   **FITZGIBBON, V.**
                             John Baron Fitzgibbon.
                             Peerage, p. 65.

1794 1 Mar.   **MACARTNEY, E.**
                             George Viscount Macartney.
                             CP, viii, 324.

1794 2 Mar.   **ELY, E.**
                             Charles Viscount Loftus.
                             Peerage, p. 65.

1794 24 Oct.   **GRAVES, B.**
Thomas Graves.
LP printed in *Claims to Vote*, ii, 406–07.

1794 14 Nov.   **BRIDPORT, B.**
Sir Alexander Hood, Kt.
Remainder, failing heirs male, to Samuel Hood and heirs male, failing whom to heirs male of Alexander Hood.
LJ, xlix, 1140.

1795 12 June   **CLARE, E.**
John Viscount Fitzgibbon.
Peerage, p. 66.

1795 12 June   **SOMERTON, B.**
Charles Agar, Archbishop of Cashel.
Peerage, p. 66.

1795 15 June   **YELVERTON, B.**
Barry Yelverton.
Peerage, p. 66.

1795 30 Sept.   **LEITRIM, E.**
Robert Viscount Leitrim.
Peerage, p. 66; dated 6 Oct. (*sic*) 1795 in *CP*, vii, 580.

1795 30 Sept.   **MOUNTJOY, V.**
Luke Baron Mountjoy.
Peerage, p. 66.

1795 30 Sept.   **KILWARDEN, B.**
Anne Wolfe.
Remainder to heirs male by husband.
List, p. 52a.

1795 1 Oct.   **LUCAN, E.**
Charles Baron Lucan.
Peerage, p. 66.

1795 1 Oct.   **CASTLEREAGH, V.**
Robert Baron Londonderry.
Peerage, p. 66.

1795 1 Oct.   **LONGUEVILLE, B.**
Richard Longfield.
Peerage, p. 66.

1795 1 Oct.   **LAVINGTON, B.**
Sir Ralph Payne, Kt.
List, p. 52a.

1795 2 Oct.   **OXMANTOWN, V.**
Laurence Harman Baron Oxmantown.
Peerage, p. 66; dated 6 (*sic*) Oct. 1795 in *CP*, xi,
168.

1795 3 Oct.   **O'NEILL, V.**
John Baron O'Neill.
Peerage, p. 66.

1795 3 Oct.   **RANCLIFFE, B.**
Thomas Boothby Parkyns.
List, p. 52a.

1795 4 Oct.   **BANDON, V.**
Francis Baron Bandon.
Peerage, p. 66.

1796 9 July   **HUNTINGFIELD, B.**
Sir Joshua Vanneck, Bart.
List, p. 52b; dated 7(*sic*) July 1796 in *CP*, vi, 674.

1796 11 July   **CARRINGTON, B.**
Robert Smith.
List, p. 52b.

1796 8 Aug.   **LONDONDERRY, E.**
Robert Viscount Castlereagh.
Peerage, p. 67.

1796 19 Oct.   **ROSSMORE, B.**
Robert Cuninghame.
Remainder, failing heirs male, to Henry Alexander
Jones, Warner William Westenra and Henry Westenra and
heirs male.
Peerage, p. 66; dated 27 (*sic*) Oct. 1796 in *List*,
p. 52b.

1797 16 Mar. **KEITH, B.**
Hon. Sir George Keith Elphinstone, Kt.
Remainder, failing heirs male, to daughter Margaret
Mercer Elphinstone and heirs male.
List, p. 52b.

1797 17 Mar. **HOTHAM, B.**
William Hotham.
Remainder, failing heirs male, to heirs male of father.
List, p. 52b.

1797 24 Mar. **BANTRY, B.**
Richard White.
Peerage, p. 68.

1797 20 Nov. **BELMORE, E.**
Armar Lowry Viscount Belmore.
List, p. 52c; LP printed in *Claims to Vote*, ii, 135–7;
dated 2 (*sic*) Nov. 1797 in *Peerage*, p. 67.

1797 20 Nov. **DONOUGHMORE, V.**
Richard Hely Baron Donoughmore.
Remainder, failing heirs male, to heirs male of mother.
Peerage, p. 67.

1797 20 Nov. **CREMORNE, B.**
Thomas Viscount Cremorne.
Remainder, failing heirs male, to nephew Richard
Dawson and heirs male.
List, p. 52c.

1797 21 Nov. **CONYNGHAM, E.**; Mount Charles, V.
Henry Viscount Conyngham.
Peerage, p. 67; dated 27 Dec. (*sic*) 1797 in *CP*, iii, 411.

1797 21 Nov. **CARLETON, V.**
Hugh Baron Carleton.
Peerage, p. 67.

1797 21 Nov. **SUNDERLIN, B.**
Richard Baron Sunderlin.
Remainder, failing heirs male, to brother Edmond
Malone and heirs male.
List, p. 52c.

1797 22 Nov.   **LANDAFF, E.**
                      Francis Viscount Landaff.
                      Peerage, p. 67.

1797 22 Nov.   **FERRARD, V.**
                      Margaretta Amelia Baroness Oriel.
                      List, p. 52c.

1797 22 Nov.   **TYRAWLEY, B.**
                      James Cuffe.
                      Peerage, p. 67.

1797 23 Nov.   **CALEDON, V.**
                      James Baron Caledon.
                      Peerage, p. 67; dated 22 (*sic*) Nov. 1797 in *List*, p. 52c.

1797 23 Nov.   **MONCK, B.**
                      Charles Stanley Monck.
                      Peerage, p. 67.

1797 24 Nov.   **NORWOOD, B.**
                      Grace Toler.
                      List, p. 52c.

1797 25 Nov.   **KILCONNEL, B.**
                      William Power Keating Trench.
                      Peerage, p. 68.

1797 26 Nov.   **TULLAMORE, B.**
                      Charles William Bury.
                      Peerage, p. 67.

1797 27 Nov.   **HEADLEY, B.**
                      Sir George Allanson Winn, Bart.
                      List, p. 52c; LP printed in *LJ*, lxxxix, 388–9.

1798 14 Feb.   **KENMARE, V.**; Castlerosse, B.
                      Sir Valentine Browne, Bart.
                      Peerage, p. 68; *CP*, vii, 115.

1798 3 Mar.   **TEIGNMOUTH, B.**
                      Sir John Shore, Bart.
                      List, p. 52d.

1798 4 Mar.   **HOLMES, B.**
Leonard Holmes.
List, p. 52d.

1798 9 Mar.   **CROFTON, B.**
Anne Lady Crofton.
Remainder to heirs male by late husband.
List, p. 52d; dated 8 (*sic*) Mar. 1798 in *CP*, iii, 543.

1798 12 Mar.   **FFRENCH, B.**
Rose Ffrench.
Remainder to heirs male by late husband.
List, p. 52d.

1798 2 July   **KILWARDEN, B.**
Arthur Wolfe.
Peerage, p. 68; dated 3 (*sic*) July 1798 in *CP*, vii, 267.

1799 24 Apr.   **DUBLIN, E.**
Prince Edward.
Also grant of dukedom of Kent and Strathearn
(GB).
C 231/13 p. 221; LP 39 Geo. III, pt. 7 (C 66/3958)
no. 3.

1799 24 Apr.   **ARMAGH, E.**
Prince Ernest Augustus.
Also grant of dukedom of Cumberland and Teviotdale
(GB).
C 231/13 p. 221; LP 39 Geo. III, pt. 7 (C 66/3958)
no. 2.

1799 9 Nov.   **HENLEY, B.**
Sir Morton Eden, Kt.
List, p. 52f.

1799 23 Dec.   **WELLESLEY, M.**
Richard Earl of Mornington and Baron Wellesley
(GB).
List, p. 52f; dated 2 (*sic*) Dec. 1799 in *CP*, ix, 237.

1800 4 Apr.   **WHITWORTH, B.**
Charles Whitworth.
CP, xii(2), 619.

1800 31 July   **CASTLE COOTE, B.**
                      Charles Henry Earl of Mountrath.
                      Remainder, failing heirs male, to kinsman Charles
                      Henry Coote and heirs male.
                      List, p. 52g.

1800 31 July   **LANGFORD, B.**
                      Hon. Clotworthy Rowley.
                      List, p. 52g.

1800 31 July   **DE BLAQUIERE, B.**
                      Sir John de Blaquiere, Bart.
                      Peerage, p. 69; LP printed in *Claims to Vote*, ii, 258–9;
                      dated 30 (*sic*) July 1800 in *CP*, iv, 108.

1800 31 July   **FRANKFORT DE MONTMORENCY, B.**
                      Lodge Evans Morres.
                      Peerage, p. 69.

1800 31 July   **DUFFERIN AND CLANEBOYE, B.**
                      Dorcas Lady Blackwood.
                      Remainder to heirs male by late husband.
                      List, p. 52g.

1800 31 July   **HENNIKER, B.**
                      Sir John Henniker, Bart.
                      List, p. 52g.

1800 31 July   **NEWCOMEN, B.**
                      Charlotte Lady Gleadowe-Newcomen.
                      List, p. 52g.

1800 31 July   **ADARE, B.**
                      Sir Valentine Richard Quin, Bart.
                      Peerage, p. 69.

1800 31 July   **VENTRY, B.**
                      Sir Thomas Mullins, Bart.
                      Peerage, p. 69.

1800 31 July   **ENNISMORE, B.**
                      William Hare.
                      List, p. 52g.

1800 31 July

WALLSCOURT, B.
Joseph Henry Blake.
Remainder, failing heirs male, to heirs male of father.
Peerage, p. 69.

1800 31 July

MOUNT SANDFORD, B.
Henry Moore Sandford.
Remainder, failing heirs male, to brothers and heirs male.
List, p. 52g.

1800 31 July

DUNALLEY, B.
Ralph Sadleir Prittie.
List, p. 52g; LP printed in *Claims to Vote*, ii, 323–5.

1800 31 July

TARA, B.
John Preston.
Peerage, p. 69.

1800 31 July

HARTLAND, B.
Maurice Mahon.
List, p. 52g.

1800 31 July

CLANMORRIS, B.
John Bingham.
List, p. 52g.

1800 28 Aug.

O'NEILL, E.; Raymond, V.
Charles Henry Viscount O'Neill.
List, p. 52g; dated – (*sic*) Aug. 1800 in *CP*, x, 62.

1800 29 Aug.

BANDON, E.; Bernard, V.
Francis Viscount Bandon.
List, p. 52g; LP printed in *LJ*, lxxxviii, 574–5.

1800 19 Dec.

LECALE, B.
Lord Charles James Fitzgerald.
List, p. 52h; dated 27 (*sic*) Dec. 1800 in *CP*, vii, 503.

1800 20 Dec.

RADSTOCK, B.
Hon. Sir William Waldegrave, Kt.
LJ, lxxxix, 72; dated 29 (*sic*) Dec. 1800 in *CP*, x, 722 and 17 Aug. 1801 (*sic*) in *List*, p. 52h.

1800 21 Dec.　　　**GLENBERVIE, B.**
　　　　　　　　　　Sylvester Douglas.
　　　　　　　　　　List, p. 52h; dated 30 Nov. (*sic*) 1800 in *CP*, v, 668.

1800 22 Dec.　　　**NORBURY, B.**
　　　　　　　　　　John Toler.
　　　　　　　　　　List, p. 52h; dated 27 (*sic*) Dec. 1800 in *CP*, ix, 566.

1800 23 Dec.　　　**GARDNER, B.**
　　　　　　　　　　Alan Gardner.
　　　　　　　　　　List, p. 52h.

1800 26 Dec.　　　**NUGENT, B.**
　　　　　　　　　　Mary Elizabeth Marchioness of Buckingham.
　　　　　　　　　　Remainder to second son Lord George Nugent
　　　　　　　　　　Grenville and heirs male.
　　　　　　　　　　List, p. 52h.

1800 27 Dec.　　　**ASHTOWN, B.**
　　　　　　　　　　Frederick Trench.
　　　　　　　　　　Remainder, failing heirs male, to heirs male of father.
　　　　　　　　　　List, p. 52h; LP printed in *LJ*, lxxxvii, 320–21.

1800 28 Dec.　　　**CLARINA, B.**
　　　　　　　　　　Eyre Massey.
　　　　　　　　　　List, p. 52h.

1800 29 Dec.　　　**THOMOND, M.**
　　　　　　　　　　Murrough Earl of Inchiquin.
　　　　　　　　　　Remainder, failing heirs male, to brothers and heirs
　　　　　　　　　　male.
　　　　　　　　　　List, p. 52h; LP printed in *Claims to Vote*, iii, 117–19.

1800 29 Dec.　　　**CLANRICARDE, E.**
　　　　　　　　　　John Thomas Earl of Clanricarde.
　　　　　　　　　　Remainder, failing heirs male, to daughters and heirs
　　　　　　　　　　male.
　　　　　　　　　　List, p. 52h.

1800 29 Dec.　　　**LIMERICK, V.**
　　　　　　　　　　Edmond Henry Baron Glentworth.
　　　　　　　　　　List, p. 52h.

1800 29 Dec.　　　**ERRIS, B.**
　　　　　　　　　　Hon. Robert Edward King.
　　　　　　　　　　List, p. 52h.

1800 30 Dec. **HEADFORT, M.**
Thomas Earl of Bective.
List, p. 52h.

1800 30 Dec. **CASTLE STEWART, E.**
Andrew Thomas Viscount Castle Stewart.
List, p. 52h.

1800 30 Dec. **SOMERTON, V.**
Charles Baron Somerton.
List, p. 52h.

1800 31 Dec. **SLIGO, M.**
John Denis Earl of Altamont.
List, p. 52h; dated 29 (*sic*) Dec. 1800 in *CP*, xii(1), 24.

1800 31 Dec. **DONOUGHMORE, E.**
Richard Hely Viscount Donoughmore.
Remainder, failing heirs male, to heirs male of mother.
List, p. 52h; LP printed in *LJ*, lxxxvi, 228–9.

1801 1 Jan. **ELY, M.**
Charles Earl of Ely.
List, p. 52h.

1801 1 Jan. **CALEDON, E.**
James Viscount Caledon.
List, p. 52h; dated 29 Dec. 1800 (*sic*) in *CP*, ii, 485.

1801 1 Jan. **AVONMORE, V.**
Barry Baron Yelverton.
List, p. 52h; dated 29 Dec. 1800 (*sic*) in *CP*, i, 362.

1801 2 Jan. **KENMARE, E.**; Castlerosse, V.
Valentine Viscount Kenmare.
List, p. 52h.

1801 2 Jan. **LONGUEVILLE, V.**
Richard Baron Longueville.
List, p. 52h; dated 29 Dec. 1800 (*sic*) in *CP*, viii, 129.

1801 3 Jan. **BANTRY, V.**
Richard Baron Bantry.
List, p. 52h; dated 29 Dec. 1800 (*sic*) in *CP*, i, 415.

1801 5 Jan.	**MONCK, V.**
	Charles Stanley Baron Monck.
	List, p. 52h.
1801 6 Jan.	**DUNLO, V.**
	William Power Keating Baron Kilconnel.
	List, p. 52h; dated 3 (*sic*) Jan. 1801 in *CP*, iii, 218.
1801 7 Jan.	**CHARLEVILLE, V.**
	Charles William Baron Tullamore.
	List, p. 52h; dated 29 Dec. 1800 (*sic*) in *CP*, iii, 141.
1801 8 Jan.	**KILWARDEN, V.**
	Arthur Baron Kilwarden.
	List, p. 52h; dated 29 Dec. 1800 (*sic*) in *CP*, vii, 267.
1803 20 Jan.	**LIMERICK, E.**
	Edmond Henry Viscount Limerick.
	List, p. 52l; dated 1 (*sic*) Jan. 1803 in *CP*, vii, 633.
1803 20 Jan.	**CLANCARTY, E.**
	William Power Keating Viscount Dunlo.
	List, p. 52l; dated 11 Feb. (*sic*) 1803 in *CP*, iii, 218.
1803 11 Feb.	**NEWCOMEN, V.**
	Charlotte Baroness Newcomen.
	CP, ix, 538.
1806 1 Feb.	**GOSFORD, E.**
	Arthur Viscount Gosford.
	List, p. 52n.
1806 3 Feb.	**ROSSE, E.**
	Laurence Harman Viscount Oxmantown.
	Remainder, failing heirs male to nephew Sir Laurence Parsons, Bart. and heirs male.
	List, p. 52n.
1806 4 Feb.	**NORMANTON, E.**
	Charles Viscount Somerton.
	List, p. 52n.
1806 5 Feb.	**CHARLEVILLE, E.**
	Charles William Viscount Charleville.
	List, p, 52n; LP printed in *LJ*, lxxxv, 275–6; dated 16 (*sic*) Feb. 1806 in *CP*, iii, 141.

1806 13 Feb.   **TEMPLETOWN, V.**
John Henry Baron Templetown.
List, p. 52n.

1806 25 Feb.   **RENDLESHAM, B.**
Peter Isaac Thellusson.
List, p. 52n; dated 1 (*sic*) Feb. 1806 in *CP*, x, 766.

1806 24 May   **LISMORE, V.**
Cornelius Baron Lismore.
List, p. 52n; dated 30 (*sic*) May 1806 in *CP*, viii, 81.

1806 28 May   **LORTON, V.**
Robert Edward Baron Erris.
List, p. 52n.

1810 18 May   **KILTARTON, B.**
John Prendergast Smyth.
Remainder, failing heirs male, to Charles Vereker and heirs male.
List, p. 52g; original LP in Parliamentary Archives, HL/PO/JO/10/3/294–A; dated 15 (*sic*) May 1810 in *CP*, vi, 28.

1812 21 Dec.   **CASTLEMAINE, B.**
William Handcock.
Remainder, failing heirs male, to brother Richard Handcock and heirs male.
List, p. 52s.

1812 22 Dec.   **DECIES, B.**
William Beresford, Archbishop of Tuam.
List, p. 52s.

1816 12 Jan.   **ORMOND, M.**
Walter Earl of Ormond and Baron Butler (UK).
List, p. 52u; dated – (*sic*) Jan. 1816 in *CP*, x, 164.

1816 12 Jan.   **BLESINGTON, E.**
Charles John Viscount Mountjoy.
List, p. 52u.

1816 12 Jan.   **FRANKFORT DE MONTMORENCY, V.**
Lodge Evans Baron Frankfort de Montmorency.
List, p. 52u.

1816 13 Jan.   **LONDONDERRY, M.**
Robert Earl of Londonderry.
List, p. 52u.

1816 13 Jan.   **BANTRY, E.**; Berehaven, V.
Richard Viscount Bantry.
List, p. 52u; LP printed in *LJ*, lxxxiii, 382–3; dated 22
(*sic*) Jan. 1816 in *CP*, i, 415.

1816 15 Jan.   **CONYNGHAM, M.**; Mount Charles, E.; Slane, V.
Henry Earl Conyngham.
List, p. 52u.

1816 15 Jan.   **GLENGALL, E.**; Caher, V.
Richard Baron Caher.
List, p. 52u; dated 22 (*sic*) Jan. 1816 in *CP*, v, 679.

1816 15 Jan.   **ENNISMORE AND LISTOWEL, V.**
William Baron Ennismore.
List, p. 52u.

1816 16 Jan.   **SHEFFIELD, E.**; Pevensey, V.
John Baker Baron Sheffield and Baron Sheffield (UK).
List, p. 52u; dated 22 (*sic*) Jan. 1816 in *CP*, xi, 665.

1816 16 Jan.   **GORT, V.**
John Baron Kiltarton.
Remainder, failing heirs male, to Charles Vereker and
heirs male.
List, p. 52u.

1816 3 Feb.   **MOUNT EARL, V.**
Valentine Richard Baron Adare.
CP, iv, 547.

1819 30 Jan.   **GARVAGH, B.**
George Canning.
LP printed in *LJ*, lxxxv, 274–5; dated 28 Oct. 1819
(*sic*) in *CP*, v, 623.

1819 19 Oct.   **HOWDEN, B.**
Sir John Francis Cradock, Kt.
CP, vi, 594.

George IV

1822 12 Jan. **WESTMEATH, M.**
George Thomas John Earl of Westmeath.
LJ, ciii, 261.

1822 12 Jan. **RATHDOWNE, E.**
Henry Stanley Viscount Monck.
CP, ix, 50.

1822 12 Jan. **CASTLEMAINE, V.**
William Baron Castlemaine.
CP, iii, 93.

1822 5 Feb. **LISTOWEL, E.**
William Viscount Ennismore and Listowel.
LP printed in *LJ*, lxxxviii, 382–3.

1822 5 Feb. **DUNRAVEN AND MOUNT EARL, E.**; Adare, V.
Valentine Richard Viscount Mount Earl.
LP printed in *LJ*, lxxxiii, 381–2.

1822 5 Feb. **KILMOREY, E.**; Newry and Morne, V.
Francis Viscount Kilmorey.
LJ, lxiv, 40; dated 12 Jan. (*sic*) 1822 in *CP*, vii,
263.

1822 10 Dec. **DOWNES, B.**
William Downes.
Remainder, failing heirs male, to cousin Sir Ulysses
Burgh, Kt. and heirs male.
CP, iv, 456.

1825 14 May **BLOOMFIELD, B.**
Benjamin Bloomfield.
CP, ii, 194.

1825 5 Oct. **ORMOND, M.**
James Earl of Ormond and Baron Ormond (UK).
CP, x, 165.

1825 26 Nov. **CLANRICARDE, M.**
Ulick John Earl of Clanricarde.
CP, iii, 237.

1826 27 June **FITZGERALD AND VESEY, B.**
       Catherine Fitzgerald.
       LJ, lxvi, 346; dated 31 July (*sic*) 1826 in *CP*, v, 405.

1827 23 June **NORBURY, E.**; Glandine, V.
       John Baron Norbury.
       Remainder to second son and heirs male.
       LJ, lxiii, 964; *CP*, v, 566.

William IV

1831 6 Jan. **GUILLAMORE, V.**; O'Grady, B.
       Standish O'Grady.
       Abstract, p. 11; LP printed in *LJ*, lxxxviii, 385–6; dated
       28 (*sic*) Jan. 1831 in *CP*, vi, 219.

1831 28 May **TALBOT DE MALAHIDE, B.**
       Margaret Talbot.
       Remainder to heirs male by late husband.
       LP printed in *LJ*, lxxxiii, 267–8; dated 26 (*sic*) May
       1831 in *Abstract*, p. 16.

1831 14 Sept. **RANFURLY, E.**
       Thomas Viscount Northland and Baron Ranfurly (UK).
       Abstract, p. 19.

1834 13 June **CAREW, B.**
       Robert Shapland Carew.
       Abstract, p. 47.

1836 4 May **ORANMORE AND BROWNE, B.**
       Dominick Browne.
       Abstract, p. 67.

Victoria

1845 3 June **DUNSANDLE AND CLANCONAL, B.**
       James Daly.
       LJ, lxxvii, 734; dated 6 (*sic*) June 1845 in *CP*, iv, 550.

1848 10 July   **BELLEW, B.**
Sir Patrick Bellew, Bart.
LP printed in *LJ*, lxxxviii, 387–8.

1852 11 Feb.   **CLERMONT, B.**
Thomas Fortescue.
Remainder, failing heirs male, to brother Chichester
Samuel Fortescue and heirs male.
LP printed in *LJ*, lxxxv, 537–9.

1855 14 May   **FERMOY, B.**
Edmund Burke Roche.
LP printed in *LJ*, lxxxviii, 85–6.
The House of Lords resolved 1 July 1856 that grantee
had not made out his claim to vote at elections for
representative peers (*ibid*. 336); in consequence he received
fresh LP 10 Sept. 1856.

1856 10 Sept   **FERMOY, B.**
Edmund Burke Roche.
LP printed in *LJ*, lxxxix, 312–13.

1863 14 Dec.   **ATHLUMNEY, B.**
Sir William Meredyth Somerville, Bart.
LP printed in *LJ*, xcvi, 87–8.

1868 10 Aug.   **ABERCORN, D.**; Hamilton, M.
James Marquess of Abercorn (GB) and Viscount
Strabane.
CP, i, 9.

1868 21 Dec.   **RATHDONNELL, B.**
John McClintock.
Remainder, failing heirs male, to heirs male of brother
William Bunbury McClintock Bunbury.
LP printed in *LJ*, ci, 229–30.

1898 11 Nov.   **CURZON OF KEDLESTON, B.**
Hon. George Nathaniel Curzon.
LJ, cxl, 19.

Index of Titles